AN
AMERICAN
MOMENT

Text
Bill Harris

Design
Clive Dorman

Commissioning Editor
Andrew Preston

Photo Research
Annette Lerner
Anne Stewart

Editorial
Scott Coombs
Pauline Graham

Production
Ruth Arthur
David Proffit

Director of Production
Gerald Hughes

Director of Publishing
David Gibbon

The Publishers wish to thank Black Star of New York, who provided the
majority of the photographs for this book. Particular gratitude is due to
Ben Chadwick and Anne Stewart for their invaluable assistance.

CLB 2376
© 1990 Colour Library Books Ltd, Godalming, Surrey, England
All rights reserved
This 1990 edition published by Portland House,
a division of dilithium Press, Ltd, distributed by Crown Publishers, Inc,
225 Park Avenue South, New York, New York 10003
Printed and bound in Spain.
ISBN 0 517 02214 1
h g f e d c b a

This book is dedicated to the memory of Nat Wartels

AN
AMERICAN
MOMENT

PORTLAND HOUSE

1 WASHINGTON	18 ILLINOIS	35 ALABAMA
2 IDAHO	19 INDIANA	36 FLORIDA
3 MONTANA	20 OHIO	37 GEORGIA
4 OREGON	21 NEBRASKA	38 SOUTH CAROLINA
5 CALIFORNIA	22 KANSAS	39 NORTH CAROLINA
6 NEVADA	23 MISSOURI	40 DELAWARE
7 UTAH	24 TEXAS	41 NEW JERSEY
8 WYOMING	25 OKLAHOMA	42 PENNSYLVANIA
9 COLORADO	26 ARKANSAS	43 NEW YORK STATE
10 ARIZONA	27 TENNESSEE	44 CONNECTICUT
11 NEW MEXICO	28 KENTUCKY	45 RHODE ISLAND
12 NORTH DAKOTA	29 WEST VIRGINIA	46 MASSACHUSETTS
13 MINNESOTA	30 VIRGINIA	47 NEW HAMPSHIRE
14 WISCONSIN	31 MARYLAND	48 VERMONT
15 MICHIGAN	32 DISTRICT OF COLUMBIA	49 MAINE
16 SOUTH DAKOTA	33 LOUISIANA	50 ALASKA
17 IOWA	34 MISSISSIPPI	51 HAWAII

Contents

A Montana farmer surveys his wheat harvest.

At the end of the American Revolution, a French officer who had helped in the fight decided to have a look around before going home again. What he saw amazed him.

"While I was meditating on the great process of nature, which employs fifty thousand years in rendering the earth habitable, a new spectacle … fixed my attention and excited my curiosity," he wrote. "This was the work of a single man who, in the space of a year, had cut down several acres of wood and had built himself a house in the middle of a pretty extensive territory he had already cleared. I saw for the first time what I have since observed a hundred times; for, in fact, whatever mountains I have climbed, whatever forests I have traversed, whatever bypaths I have followed, I have never traveled three miles without meeting with a new settlement, either beginning to take form or already in cultivation." He was equally impressed by the fact that "in America, a man is never alone, never an isolated being. The neighbors are everywhere to be found."

It was an early moment in the development of America, and if two centuries later it's a rare American who would spend a year clearing a forest and building his own house (and we sometimes feud with neighbors whose kids and pets spill out of their own territory) his description still lurks deep in the country's collective self-image.

We still think of ourselves as rugged individualists, but we're incurable faddists. Though we gave the world McDonald's hamburgers, and our mothers may have been handier with a can opener than a rolling pin, we consider mom's apple pie one of the symbols of our civilization. We claim to enjoy the freedom of the wide-open spaces, but seventy-five percent of all Americans live in cities. And when we want to get out of town to smell the flowers, we go in a car that was probably made in Japan, even though the average American is fiercely proud of a technology sophisticated enough to put a man on the moon. People who run a half-dozen miles before breakfast usually drive as little as a half-mile to pick up the English muffins. And it's a rare American who would miss celebrating the Fourth of July, honoring Thomas Jefferson's declaration that "We hold these truths to be self-evident that all men are created equal, that they are endowed by their Creator with certain inalienable rights." Yet, they would be horrified if "certain" people showed up anywhere near their backyard. For all our contradictions, we're a breed that is the envy of the world. If you don't believe it, ask any American.

Describing a typical American is very much like describing a typical American landscape. There simply isn't any such thing in either case. At this moment of American history, most take as much pride in their ethnic background as in their devotion to the Stars and Stripes, though there were times in our history when immigrants worked hard at hiding their roots.

Before there was a United States, for more than a century-and-a-half in fact, even Americans who came from places like Germany and Holland learned the English language, settled in towns named for places in Britain, obeyed laws approved by the English king and even paid taxes to London. When they finally rebelled against all that, they discovered that severing political bonds is one thing, but creating a new national identity is quite another. They still spoke English, read the King James Bible, and found that their code of laws had a demonstrably English character. But they had fought a long war for their independence and if they still talked like the English, they had something new to say. Their Constitution had its roots in English law, but it owed as much to the French Enlightenment, and the mixture was exactly right to send a message to the world that freedom was a reality in this new country no matter who you were or where you came from.

They came from all over Europe, eager to work for a new life and to turn their backs on the old one. In the process, they began creating this creature we identify with today. As early as 1782, Michel-Guillaume-Jean de Crèvecœur's book, *Letters From an American Farmer*, offered a description for the less fortunate still on the other side of the Atlantic:

> What then is the American, this new man? He is either a European or the descendant of a European, hence that strange mixture of blood which you will find in no other country. I could point out to you a family whose grandfather was an Englishman, whose wife was Dutch, whose son married a French woman, and whose present four sons have wives of four different nations. He is an American who, leaving behind him all his ancient prejudices and manners, receives new ones from the new mode of life he has embraced, the new government he obeys, and the new rank he holds. He becomes an American by being received into the broad lap of our great Alma Mater. Here individuals are melted into a new race of men, whose labors and posterity will one day cause great changes in the world.

The best part was that anybody in the world could change into this new man. All that was required of any free white immigrant was to give up any hereditary titles and political allegiance to any other country, to agree to support the American Constitution and to live in the country for at least five years before applying for citizenship. There was no agency to check an applicant's past, no indoctrination, no language requirement, no questions about religion. About the only flaw was that blacks were denied the opportunity in spite of the fact that at the time the Constitution was ratified, one out of five of those who had been born in America was black.

There was also a requirement that petitioners should be "free," and though freedom was what the American experiment was all about, a huge percentage of early immigrants were denied the opportunity. They were called "redemptioners," and they arrived by the thousands looking for opportunity in the early decades of the seventeenth century. But even then opportunity had a price. They agreed in advance to work off the cost of the ocean voyage and a stake to get themselves established by working for their sponsor for a specified length of time. For many it was a lifetime, and until the debt was paid, a redemptioner was not free. And for some, the debt was passed on to their children who couldn't participate in the American Dream until it was wiped out.

The trip from the Old Country in those days never took less than seven weeks and often as many as twelve. No one traveled in the lap of luxury, but the poor were subjected to the worst possible conditions. The redemptioners had agreed to sell their souls to get to America, but they hadn't paid cash for the trip, and were forced to make do with foul water, spoiled food, overcrowding and the stench of death. Tales of pregnant women thrown overboard so their babies wouldn't add to the crowding were common; and young children under seven almost never survived the voyage. Those who did, found that their misery didn't end when the ship made port. In fact, that was when it really began. No one was allowed to leave a ship unless passage had been paid. Some redemptioners had signed agreements before leaving Europe, and were hustled off to whatever home their sponsors had decided was good enough for them. The rest were, quite simply, for sale.

Farmers, tradesman and others would board the ship to look over the available stock and negotiate with them about how long they'd be willing to work to have their passage paid. It was almost always a one-sided bargain. Anyone would promise anything to get off one of those ships. The young and healthy went first, and usually made the best bargains. Parents willingly sold their children, even knowing they'd never see them again. And youngsters whose parents died before the voyage was half over were considered responsible for the passage of the entire family. In any case, no young person could negotiate a contract that would end before the age of twenty-one.

The overwhelming majority of early redemptioners were Germans. In 1709, after a particularly harsh winter, more than thirteen thousand of them left the wine-growing region of the Rhine Valley and made their way to England. Queen Anne responded to the problem by shipping a few thousand of them off to her American colonies. They thrived in New York's Hudson Valley and found good farmland in Pennsylvania, and their letters to the folks back home gave others the idea to follow them. They went down the Rhine to Rotterdam, usually arriving there penniless after the month-long trip, and it was there that the idea of working for passage thrived. Before the flood was slowed by the Seven Years' War, more than one hundred thousand German immigrants braved the terrors of the ocean, and by 1790 more than a third of the population of Pennsylvania had come from Germany. Other colonies reported large numbers of Germans in their midst, too. And the census figures didn't include the thousands of Hessians who had deserted from the British Army after the Revolution.

But in America's search for a national identity, it was never suggested that German should become the country's official language, no matter how much the English were despised in the early days of the republic. The majority of Americans had their roots in Britain, and the influx from other countries slowed to a trickle for nearly a quarter of a century after the American government was established, ending for all time any debate that we would be anything but an English-speaking nation.

At this moment in America's history, there is a strong groundswell for making Spanish at the very least a second language; and considering the millions in America for whom it is the only language, it seems like an idea whose time has come. The Census Bureau says it counted 5.2 million Hispanic households in 1986, up from 4.8 million the year before and 3.6 million in 1980. But "households" can be a misleading term. The typical Mexican-American family has 4.5 members; and a 1970 survey of Puerto Rican families living in New York City said that more than ten percent of them included seven or more children. Confounding the statistics even more is the fact that many Spanish-speaking people in America are undocumented aliens. But no matter how you look at it, it's safe to say that enough Americans speak Spanish to give the rest of us an incentive to try to understand what they're saying.

Defenders of the language often point out that as each new ethnic group arrives, it is eventually assimilated into the society and at least the second generation signals the accomplishment by speaking English. But Spanish-speaking Americans are not a "new" ethnic group. On the contrary, it is one of the oldest we have.

In the 1820s, when the so-called Anglo-Americans began arriving in places we call New Mexico and California and spread out into Texas and Arizona, they were moving into a foreign country that had been settled by Spanish-speaking Mexicans in the sixteenth century. The English-speaking minority were required to become citizens of Mexico, to learn Spanish and to convert to Catholicism. But they were all rugged individualists, and in 1835 they staged a revolution in Texas and formed the Lone Star Republic a year later. By then they outnumbered the Spanish-speaking settlers there by about six to one. But in other parts of New Spain, especially California and New Mexico, the Anglos were very much a minority group. It eventually took a war with Mexico to make them part of the United States, and the treaty that ended it gave the Spanish-speaking segments of the population the right to stay and the option of becoming American citizens. Later, the pressure to build a transcontinental railroad across pockets of territory the Mexican government had retained resulted in the purchase of some thirty thousand square miles of southern New Mexico and Arizona. Its Spanish-speaking population became American citizens as soon as the check was signed.

More Mexicans settled in California during the 1849 Gold Rush, and when it was over, many stayed. And in the next half-century thousands migrated into Arizona and Texas. It was estimated that by the beginning of the twentieth century, there were more than a half-million Mexicans living in the Southwest, and in the next twenty years, the number doubled. Restrictive laws and the Great Depression of the 1930s reversed the tide, and though quotas have been established, and thousands deported, the movement across the border is probably stronger than ever.

Mexican-Americans began settling the Southwest, but in this century, they have followed the harvests as migrant farm workers into every corner of the United States. The traditional pattern has taken them up the West Coast into the Pacific Northwest and then across to the Eastern Seaboard and back to the Southwest. Each year, more and more of them find opportunities along the way and resettle, with the result that there are Mexican-American communities in nearly every state.

And if they've changed their addresses, they've also changed their status. Former migrant farmers have taken white collar jobs, and more than twenty percent of them are classed as skilled workers. The number is growing fast, and the people who called themselves "Chicanos" in the 1960s are hard at work improving opportunities in education, in employment, in the political process.

The entire Hispanic community is benefiting from their efforts, but though they share a common language, all Spanish-speaking Americans can't be considered together as a single race. They're more like cousins than brothers. Mexican-Americans are a mixture of Spanish and Indian roots. Puerto Ricans, on the other hand, have no Indian blood. When their island became a Spanish colony in 1493, the Indians who were there first fell victim to the diseases of civilization and were almost completely eliminated in less than twenty years. The conquerors solved the labor problem by importing black slaves, and their descendants are the product of African and Spanish roots.

Another major difference is that all Puerto Ricans are American citizens, free to travel anywhere on the mainland without any of the usual restrictions that hamper immigrants, including other Hispanics. They're faced with the same culture shock when they migrate north, but in spite of it, they are more likely to resettle in places like Chicago or New York, which is home to more than half the mainland Puerto Rican population.

The first Puerto Ricans in the United States were political exiles who arrived in the nineteeth century, and most of them went home again when the island became a U.S. possession after the Spanish-American War. But the ships that took them there went back to New York with immigrants looking for opportunity. Severe hurricanes in 1928 and 1932 wiped out hundreds of coffee plantations and thousands of jobs, and young people took advantage of their status as American citizens to improve their lives. The American government, which has controlled Puerto Rico since 1898, gave them independence, and with it citizenship, in 1917. But mass migration didn't begin until after World War II, when the airplane made it convenient to go from San Juan to New York in a matter of hours. There was a substantial Puerto Rican community in the New York area by then, and the combination of having friends and family at the receiving end, massive unemployment at home and a low cost way to turn their lives around lured them by the thousands.

Like other groups before them, the Puerto Ricans by and large came to America with the idea of making their fortune and then going home again. But unlike other groups, many have succeeded. The number of Puerto Ricans living on the mainland today is equal to about a third of population of the island, but almost another third living in Puerto Rico right now have lived on the mainland at some point in their lives. But none of them has found life in the United States a bed of roses. Though they have the rights of citizenship, Puerto Rico is not a state, and they are generally treated as second-class citizens, overwhelmed on one hand by the more numerous and more influential Latinos and on the other by the black civil rights movement which has shunned them, even though the Census Bureau, which concerns itself with the differences among Americans, classifies Puerto Ricans as black. But there are hopeful signs within the older established communities where families are into the second and third generation as mainlanders. The men are more likely to be professionals and their families more stable. They have higher educational backgrounds and higher incomes than the newer arrivals, a trend many experts feel says good things about the future of Puerto Ricans in the United States.

And there is plenty of precedent in other ethnic groups to prove the theory.

Like other ethnic groups, they are largely Roman Catholic, but their brand of Catholicism has been difficult to transplant. They find churches that speak their language, but most are forced to share their religion with others from Central America as well as their English-speaking neighbors, and the sense of community the church gave them at home is missing. It's a problem as old as the United States itself. The Constitution was quite specific that there was to be no state religion, but America was clearly a Protestant nation to the men who wrote the document.

Until after the War of 1812, when the country began growing again, an entire generation of Americans had seen almost no immigration. When the tide of humanity started to overwhelm them in the 1830s, they began grumbling about the strangers in their midst, and questions about what it really takes to be an American began to take on an ugly edge. And at the heart of almost every discussion was not so much that their new neighbors spoke strange languages, wore odd clothes and followed customs that were vaguely un-American, but that they had a different way of talking to God. More and more of the newcomers were Roman Catholics. Catholics had been migrating to America from earliest Colonial times, but they were still practically non-existent in most parts of the country. It provided fertile ground for prejudice. Rather than singling out any one nationality as an object of hate, it was much simpler to focus on the religion so many of them had in common. That way, a man could tell his pals down at the tavern that he had nothing at all against Poles, for instance, but he couldn't abide the idea of a bunch of papists kowtowing to a higher authority than the government of the United States.

Before long the tavern discussions led to the establishment of "native American" clubs and associations. And soon after, the venom even began coming from the pulpits of Protestant churches. The earliest settlers had established their colonies with high-sounding religious principles and their descendants inherited the idea not only that America was the key to God's plan for the world but that He had ordained them to carry it out. The idea reached a fever pitch in the 1830s as the country began expanding westward and religious revivalists followed the new settlers with reassurances that God was with them all the way. Christ was coming back to earth, they were told, and when He did, He was going to run His kingdom from America. It was their sacred responsibility to make themselves ready, to forsake demon rum and to be vigilant against the rising power of the Catholic church in their midst. It was obvious to the evangelists that the devil himself had sent all those Catholics to provide a counterbalance to the coming millenium. If their audiences weren't all quite ready for total abstinence, they were more than willing to give a total commitment to defending their country against the ravages of Rome.

Their enthusiasm eventually led to the formation of a political party that called itself, ironically, the Know-Nothings. It was dedicated to changing the naturalization laws to exclude Catholics completely and increase the residency requirement to twenty-one years. It also called for the exclusion of Catholics and foreign-born citizens from holding public office. And if their ideas seem absurd today, they were taken quite seriously by our ancestors. The Know-Nothings became the majority party in a half-dozen states and had seventy-five members in Congress in 1855. But by then, America had other things on its mind, and the party finally faded away. The country was coming apart at the seams over the question of whether it was a single nation or an amalgam of states. And at the heart of that controversy was an issue that had been lurking in the background from the beginning, the right to own slaves.

Even then, the debate about what constituted an American overlooked the Afro-Americans in our midst. Even Thomas Jefferson, who declared that "all men are created equal," drew the line at slaves on his own and other Southern plantations. For the most part the African slave trade was originally destined for the Caribbean and South America, and the majority of the less than five hundred thousand black slaves who arrived in North America came in the second half of the eighteenth century. By the time slavery was

abolished, the importation of blacks had been illegal for nearly sixty years, and there were few, if any, who weren't native-born Americans. But if they were free, it was only a technicality. It took a full five years after emancipation to pass a Constitutional amendment that recognized their citizenship, and another two to guarantee their right to vote. In the years just before the Civil War when large numbers of free blacks began settling in Northern states, only five of the New England states, where the abolition movement began, allowed them to vote; and in New York, the only other place where the right was extended, the franchise was denied to any black who couldn't post a two hundred fifty dollar bond. Most other states also denied them the right to serve on juries or in the militia or to intermarry with other races. In Ohio, they were required to post a bond of five hundred dollars to establish residency, but they were denied any other rights beyond the privilege of living there.

Emancipation changed laws, but not attitudes, and freed slaves who drifted north and mingled with blacks whose families had been free for generations found that assimilating into a white society was going to be more of a nightmare than a dream. Joining the black establishment, such as it was, wasn't going to be all that easy either. About all the two groups had in common was the color of their skin. But they had another bond, and it became a strong part of the American fabric that is still very much with us.

In 1781, the same year the Constitution was ratified, a pair of black ministers in Philadelphia took advantage of the freedom it promised by organizing the freed slaves who were members of St. George's Methodist church and began holding services especially for them in a church they called Mother Bethel. Others followed their lead, and by 1816, when the African Methodist Episcopal church grew from Bethel's roots, there were black ministries in every major Northern city. In those early years, all of the ministers had themselves lived as slaves, and their style of worship was a combination of African tradition and European beliefs. It was an entirely new religion based more on the community of men than man's individual relationship with God that had been at the core of the Protestant movement. Members of the congregation were encouraged to join in with the preacher when the spirit moved them, and there was a heavier emphasis on music than in the white churches, along with a stronger call for togetherness. And in the late 1860s, newly freed slaves found a new sense of community in the familiar surroundings of their churches, even if they found the land of the free a generally hostile place.

Much of the leadership in the black community, both in the North and the South, came directly from the churches. The ministers provided a political force and gave their followers a voice in the white man's institutions. The Civil War was still being fought when they joined together to form the National Equal Rights League, and by the time the war ended, they were already at work to end segregation in transportation, schools and other public accommodations. They were largely successful, too, and during the late 1860s and early 1870s, civil rights laws blossomed in state after state. But as fast as the laws were passed, ways were found to get around them. Some states amended their own constitutions to avoid the implications of the new amendments to the federal constitution, and finally, in 1896 the United States Supreme Court ruled that it was acceptable to keep the races "separate but equal." The matter rested there until 1948 when President Harry S. Truman issued an order to desegregate the armed forces and set the stage for a new civil rights movement that took another twenty years to accomplish goals that had been established a hundred years earlier.

But if the early black leadership was able to produce at least token integration, no amount of political persuasion could solve the problem of how to earn a living. Most freed slaves understood farming, but few had learned any other trades. During the Civil War, the Union Army took over Southern plantations and resettled freed slaves on them. When General Sherman marched across Georgia, he promised the former slaves who helped him that each would be given forty acres and a mule in return for their services. But when the fighting stopped and all was finally forgiven between North and South, most of the planters got their land back and wartime promises to the blacks were forgotten. Still, someone had to work the land, and most of the old plantations were subdivided into small farms. They were leased to blacks, who turned over a percentage of their crop, often as much as two-thirds, to the landlord. Very few were ever able to get far enough ahead to even think about actually owning the land they worked, and right up to the start of the Second World War, most blacks, in the Deep South at any rate, were poor sharecroppers, no better off than the slaves who preceded them.

Many broke the chain by moving off the land and into the cities, but until the heavy waves of immigration began slowing in the pre-World War I years, they weren't able to compete against newcomers from Europe, most of whom had arrived with experience in jobs that needed to be filled. But even if jobs were scarce and blacks were forced to live in their own part of town, life in the city was less restrictive than in a sharecropper's cabin, and if those who had migrated to Northern cities found prejudice, there was less outright hostility to deal with than they had found when they attempted to relocate in the cities of the South. They lived in ghettoes, usually paying higher than average rent for less than average facilities, but they lived together as a social unit, and the togetherness gave them a cultural identity that has eventually found its way into the American mainstream.

Almost as soon as the Civil War was over, the churches began establishing funds to create colleges for blacks and by the beginning of the new century, about fifty of them were thriving, giving college degrees to young people whose parents were still illiterate. Money was also provided for secondary schools for their younger brothers and sisters, and by the 1920s the illiteracy rate among blacks was cut in half. The ability to read created a demand for newspapers within the community, and they, in turn, provided income for black writers and poets who were on their way to providing a new facet in American literature. Blacks began finding new careers in the theater around the same time. But the big black cultural explosion of the 1920s came out of the ghetto with tapping feet and smiles of pure pleasure. It gave us an art form that many feel is as all-American as anything this country has ever produced, the music we call jazz and its first cousin, the blues. As the black writer W.E.B. Du Bois told us, "there is no true American music but the wild-sweet melodies of the Negro slave." And we respond in the style of language the Afro-Americans have given us: "You ain't just whistlin' Dixie!"

Almost all of American popular music, from the theater songs of the 1930s to the big band sounds of the 1940s through rock-n-roll and rhythm-and-blues, has its roots in the black tradition. But musical America has broader horizons. The music we support, in numbers far beyond our love of sports, is as varied as the backgrounds of the American people.

In the nineteenth century, when the line between rich and poor was becoming more sharply defined, the poor supported music halls and the rich looked down on them from boxes at the opera. Grand opera was considered a hallmark of culture, even if one didn't understand the language. The statement one made by sitting through an opera didn't require understanding, just a look of rapt attention and an occasional shout of "bravo!" In colonial times, Americans preferred their operas sung in English, but according to at least one legend, they switched to the original languages because of a popular soprano who didn't want to offend their tender morals. Apparently, when she came to a risqué part of a libretto, she would switch to Italian so her audiences wouldn't be subjected to things she felt they probably shouldn't hear. Eventually they came to like the sound, and grand opera in America went back to its glorious roots. But if they liked the sound of Italian in an opera house, nineteenth-century Americans didn't especially like hearing it in their city streets.

There weren't many Italians on the American scene in colonial times. In fact, there wasn't even an Italy in the sense that we know it today. When America was being settled, it was a collection of city states that were usually at war with one another. The powerful ones in the north, which provided a trickle of seventeenth-century immigrants to America, were ultimately responsible for the *Risorgimento*, which united the country in 1870, five years after the end of the American Civil War. But even before then, about fifteen thousand had arrived, and though they settled in every part of the country, the majority found their way to California. The 1849 Gold Rush had a lot to do with it, but so did the climate. Most of the early Italian immigrants were farmers and sunny California looked more like home than any other part of North America.

After the Risorgimento, southern Italians began arriving by the thousands. Until then, they had been dominated by foreign governments at home and lived under a feudal system that reduced them to lives of poverty, and America provided them with an opportunity to change the trend. Most of those who made the trip were young men who left their families behind and ventured abroad to earn a fortune, after which they planned to go home and live in comparative luxury. Many succeeded. At the turn of the century, every two Italian immigrants arriving in America were passed by one on the way home. They often came back when their nest egg was used up, some as many as two or three times, and most eventually brought their families and settled down. Those who did usually moved to neighborhoods in the big cities of the Northeast where they could find jobs in factories and housing near enough to walk to.

The heaviest period of Italian immigration was in the first decade of the twentieth century, when more than two million came. Almost all of them landed in New York, and the majority stayed there; but Philadelphia, Boston, Chicago and Baltimore absorbed thousands, too, and each has its own distinct Italian neigborhood even today. They also migrated to New Orleans, where Sicilian immigrants had been settling since before the Civil War; and to San Francisco, where Northern Italians had established themselves as an important part of the business community for more than a generation.

But if there were farmers and fishermen, candy-makers, barbers and restaurateurs in the Italian community, the stereotype that still exists paints the early twentieth-century Italian-American as a construction worker. It's true that the majority were laborers, but so were other immigrant groups. But the Italians had an institution that made the pigeonholing inevitable: the men they called *padrones*.

By a stretch of the imagination, they could be classed along with employment agencies, because bringing men and jobs together was what they claimed to do. At first they met arriving ships and offered jobs to immigrants who knew nothing about their new country and not a word of English. Eventually they hired agents back in Italy to recruit men for a construction industry that desperately needed men. If a man had a family, that was fine with the padrone, there was work for all. The kids could at least shine shoes and their mothers could work in factories. The recruiter was entitled to a commission, of course, which the immigrants called a *bossatura* and to them, paying the "boss" became as American as the pay envelope itself. And if the need to pay continued for the length of the job, the money also covered other services such as finding them a place to live, settling disputes with neighbors who didn't understand them and generally steering them through the strange customs in this strange, new land. Eventually, the padrones outlived their usefulness, largely because the children of the immigrants took to America like fish to water and worked hard at turning their backs on the Old World.

In the world their parents left behind, the family unit was the cornerstone of the society. The father was the unquestionable head of the household and responsible for making decisions and enforcing them. The mother was usually the peacemaker between her husband and their children, but she was as much under his rule as they were. Boys were sent out to work as soon as they were able, and turned every lira they earned over to their fathers. Girls stayed home to learn the domestic routine that would rule their lives when they got married. All the children were expected to marry the person their parents selected for them, and once they did, the cycle started all over again. Family honor was the highest priority of their lives, and no one trusted anyone outside their immediate family. It was acceptable to call on a distant cousin for help when it was needed, but only if the need was urgent.

In America, things were different. Fathers expected their children to behave as they had when they were children, but as the younger generation began mixing with kids outside their neighborhood, they picked up radical new ideas. They learned English, which their parents often didn't, and that gave them a knowledge of the new country's ways. The knowledge gave them power and, like it or not, fathers began losing the authority they had taken for granted. Boys still worked, but rebelled at turning their whole paycheck over to the family. And in an even stronger break with tradition, girls went to work, too. Having their own money gave them independence, but going out to work each day also gave them a chance to broaden their matrimonial horizons. They still respected their family's wishes and almost never married outside the Italian community, but the choice was in their hands for the first time. And in the next generation, they would see their children intermarry into other ethnic groups and in some rare cases, even outside the Catholic church, a thought that horrified their grandfathers.

Over time, even Italian-Americans who didn't learn English found themselves speaking a new brand of Italian which wouldn't have been understood back in Palermo. Among the differences, a grocery store was called a *grosseria* , and the word *genitore*, which meant "parent" back in Italy, came to mean "janitor" in Italian America. But the majority worked hard to learn English and to adjust to American ways. They clung to the customs and rhythms of life they had followed in their former life, and most important, they kept the Old World in their kitchens, which has given all America a strong taste for such things as salami and spaghetti, olive oil and pizza. But even there, home cooking constituted a kind of Americanization for the early Italian immigrants. Back home, their diet had consisted almost entirely of bread and pasta, with meat and chicken reserved only for special holidays. In the New World, every day was a holiday around the kitchen table. And the best part is that they've shared it with all of us.

The Italian religious feast days are still celebrated in most major American cities with carnivals and processions, native costumes and dances and enough rich food to make you want to reach for the Alka-Seltzer just thinking about it. They all have their roots in the Italian Catholic church, but a great many Italian immigrants who kept the traditions alive had become Protestants when they became Americans. Their reasons were more political than theological, and in their hearts their new religion was no substitute for the old. When Italy was unified, the Papal states in the center of the peninsula bitterly opposed the movement, and natives of the south, whose families desperately needed the benefits of Risorgimento, felt that the church had turned on them. In return, many turned their backs on Rome. There was another reason, too. Of all the things that were different about America, number one on the list for most Italians was the Catholic church. By the time they began arriving in significant numbers, the church had become dominated by the Irish, and, to the Italians at least, they were cold and puritanical and took all the joy out of their religion. Of course, the Irish didn't see it that way at all.

Catholicism had been brought to the New World by the Spanish and French, but they concentrated their efforts on converting the heathen natives. When the English came at the beginning of the seventeenth century, they systematically drove the natives out, and regarded the Catholics as heathenish themselves. It was far from fertile ground for transplanting the religion, but the English themselves had created strong seeds.

At the same time the Pilgrims set sail for the New World, Scottish settlers were migrating into Northern Ireland. Until then, the native Catholics had owned most of the land, but the Protestant strangers, with the blessings of England, confiscated the best farms and either drove out the original owners or kept them on as tenant farmers. When Oliver Cromwell took over in the 1640s, he divided what was left of the Catholics' land among his soldiers. It was then that the problems that still exist in Ireland were born. The newcomers established the Anglican church there, and passed laws that prevented Catholics from buying land or leasing any they might already own.

For many in Ireland, the only "solution" to the problem was to emigrate to America, and thousands did. In the Cromwell era, the English accelerated the process by forcing thousands of Irish to become indentured servants and move to the New World. So many arrived in the middle of the seventeenth century in fact, that Maryland, which had been founded as a haven for Catholics, and South Carolina both passed laws imposing strict quotas on Irish immigrants. But they couldn't stop the tide. At the beginning of the eighteenth century, the English government in Ireland began deporting political prisoners and others it found undesirable on prison ships bound for America.

The early New Englanders generally welcomed Irish immigrants because they needed to expand their labor pool, but they drew the line at priests in general, and Jesuits in particular. Things began to change when Irish immigrants joined up to help fight the American Revolution, and gave such a good account of themselves that the British commander-in-chief suggested that it would be a good idea to recruit fresh troops in Ireland. The English were slow to take up the suggestion, but when the French decided to send troops to help, only the officers were French. The soldiers they led had come from Ireland. Their contribution impressed the rebels, and little by little the old prejudices died. In the meantime, a small number of affluent Catholics had come to America to preserve their fortunes, and used some of their money to support new churches for their less fortunate countrymen. It was only natural that they would send to Ireland for the priests to run them, and eventually the laws that prohibited immigration by priests fell by the wayside. By the beginning of the nineteenth century, other ethnic Catholics were beginning to call for reinstatement of the laws, and a few decades later, the Germans and Italians joined together to petition the Pope to stop the tide. But they were too late. Even their combined influence was no match for the control the Irish had over the Catholic church in America.

The strong American anti-Catholic movements began to run out of steam at about the same time immigration from Ireland was reaching its peak. When the first Catholic diocese was established in New York in 1800, its bishop was American-born, but the son of Irish immigrants. And when new diocese were formed over the next several years, all of the bishops had Irish backgrounds. Naturally, they looked to Ireland for priests to run their churches and by mid-century nearly half of all the Catholic priests in America, and all of the bishops, were Irish, most of them graduates of All Hallows College in Dublin. By 1875, no one was at all surprised when John McCloskey, a son of old Erin, was named the first American cardinal. And by the beginning of the twentieth century, seventeen cardinals had been selected to represent the United States, and only four of them didn't have Irish names.

It wasn't the result of any plot or special plan. And it wasn't because the Irish were more devout Catholics than anyone else. It some ways, it was because they weren't. Like the other Europeans in America, the Irish were totally family-oriented, and beyond their families, their church was the most important tie with the lives they left behind. But though their belief was strong, they weren't inclined to go to mass every week and that, in the eyes of their priests, was a danger signal and a sign that hard work was needed. They attacked the problem with a passion, not only to save the faith, but to raise the money to keep their churches open. At the same time they created new needs for money by broadening their service to the community in the form of hospitals and orphanages and in associations to help new immigrants assimilate and survive. They were able to act as a bridge between the immigrant and native community more effectively than priests of other nationalities because in addition to their commitment to service, they also spoke the English language. They added to their strength among their parishioners by combining religion with family life. Almost no neighborhood was without a Catholic school to serve the children of the parish. They were built with small donations from

parish members and staffed by nuns, the majority of whom, like the priests and the sisters who ran the hospitals and orphanages, had come from Ireland. Some parishes were even able to fund high schools, and by the turn of the century, the church had established colleges that allowed children of immigrants access to an affordable education. But in the beginning, making education affordable wasn't their goal. In fact, most parochial schools were forced to charge tuition, which closed the door to many immigrant children. The real purpose, at first, was to get around local laws that required the reading of the Protestant Bible in public schools.

The Irish became dominant in church affairs for another good reason. They had a knack for politics, and their priests had been cultivating it for more than a generation back accross the water. In the face of English oppression, churchmen turned to politics and encouraged their flocks to do the same. When they did, it was a heady experience, and when they came to America, they were better prepared than any other ethnic group to take on the Establishment at rallies and demonstrations and through the ballot box. The Irish who arrived in the 1820s were among the first Americans who were allowed to vote without owning property, and they knew how to use the power. Eventually they broke down the barriers political associations had put in their way and in a few years they were running many of them. The Irish bosses in cities like Boston and New York were legendary, and if they feathered their own nests, they made life bearable for the people who gave them their power.

But if life became bearable, it was just barely so, especially in Boston. One of the things that made the Bay Colony unique in colonial America was that it existed for more than two centuries with a single culture. All the English colonies to the south of it welcomed just about anybody no matter where they came from. But Boston was quite content to remain English. In the first twenty years of its existence, some twenty thousand people migrated there, and just about all of them had come from England. Not only that, but most of them were Puritans, dedicated with all their hearts to success, to God and to hard work. As their numbers grew, so did the number of towns they lived in. But Boston was the hub of their universe, and no one ever dared to challenge it. Later, as they began to industrialize, the entrepreneurs looked out into the countryside, and where the poets among them saw laughing, bubbling brooks and sparkling waterfalls, they saw free energy in the form of water power. They changed old towns and built new ones, and for the first time farmers didn't have to feel guilty about not having any work to do in the wintertime. There was cloth to be woven and shoes to be made. There was work to be done.

There was so much work, in fact, they needed more people to help them do it. Then, as they felt He had done so often for them in the past, God came up with a perfect answer. In 1845, Ireland was visited by a famine that wiped out more than a million people in less than five years. Rather than starve, a million-and-a-half of them decided to leave the country. In spite of what they may have thought of old England, New England was very attractive, indeed. There were jobs there, as were the opportunities.

Within forty years, Boston had an Irish mayor. But what a terrible forty years it was for them. It was bad enough that the newcomers were Irish. One of Boston's venerable leaders wrote: "They were the scum of creation, beaten men from beaten races, representing the worst failure in the struggle for existence. … These immigrants were inferior peoples whose prolific issue threatened the very foundations of Anglo-American civilization." And he thought he was being polite. What he really wanted to say was that the newcomers were almost all Catholics, one of the things the Puritans had come to America to get away from. And with their views on birth control … well, it was only a matter of time, wasn't it?

They called these newcomers "muckers" and "micks," "blacklegs" and "greenhorns." They hired their women, whom they always called "Bridget" at best, and "Biddy" at worst, to do the dirty work in their homes for $1.50 a week. Then they kept a third to pay for the food the women ate.

By the time the Irish began arriving after the potato famine, the old-line Yankees who had originally settled Boston's North End had decided to move to the suburbs and whole neighborhoods had simply been abandoned. Irish families began moving into the big old mansions, usually at the rate of one to a room, which meant that they shared what sanitary facilities there were among dozens of whole families. And that, in turn, meant that many of them fell victim to cholera, smallpox and worse.

But if the Puritans thought they were the only ones God gave gifts to, they didn't know much about God or the Irish. One of their gifts was for survival. They believed as an article of faith that a man's reward was waiting in heaven. It helped them endure hardships even the toughest Yankee would have blanched at, because the Puritans believed just as strongly in the here and now and considered hardship as much a punishment as a test. The Irish gift for politics helped them, too. The Yankees tried to counteract it by setting up residency and literacy laws to keep them from voting. But it was only a matter of time before that trick wouldn't work any more. They used their influence to spread stories that the Irish were drunkards, people who preferred welfare to an honest day's work and, worst of all, people who couldn't be loyal to any state because any information entrusted to them would immediately be transmitted back to the Pope in Rome.

On the other side of the coin, if the Bostonians had gone to down to meet the Irish immigrants with brass bands and CARE packages, there probably still would have been trouble between them. The Irish had some experience with the "Bloody British" back home, and their new hosts were, in most cases, more British than their cousins back in Sussex. Even though without them, America might have stayed a part of the British Empire to this day, they were English and proud of it. Then there was that old problem of religion. To the Irish, being a Protestant was about the same as being a pagan; and, of course, the Puritans were Protestants to a fault. It wasn't the first time, and unfortunately not the last, that men have used the love of God to justify hate.

By the time the Irish found their political clout, Boston and other Eastern cities had changed again. While all the scrapping was going on, Italians began arriving, then Lithuanians and Poles. Germans came too, along with Portuguese, Scandinavians and French Canadians. But it was the Irish who were in control of inner city wards, and if anyone wanted a streetlight, a bucket of coal or a city job, the Irish ward boss was the man to see. And after all those years of feeling the stings of prejudice, they proved to be just as good at dishing it out. Human nature is a mysterious thing.

Almost no group that became part of the American tapestry understood prejudice as well as the Jews. It had been a way of life for them in the Old World, and when the first of them arrived in America in 1654, they felt the stings of discrimination right away. A group of twenty-three Jews were unceremoniously put ashore at New Amsterdam, and with little more ceremony, Director-General Peter Stuyvesant began writing orders to have them deported. But many of the shareholders in the Dutch West India Company, Stuyvesant's bosses, were Jewish themselves and their influence convinced the Director-General to change his mind.

They were Sephardic Jews, descended from the group that had been expelled from Spain the same year Christopher Columbus discovered America, who had wandered in the direction of Holland and England and their colonies. They were dominant in the early Jewish life of America until the eighteenth century when Ashkenazi Jews began arriving from Eastern Europe. The two groups were as different from each other as Protestants and Catholics in the Christian world. Their religious rituals were totally different, their pronunciation of Hebrew varied and their basic concepts of community life were at odds with each other. They had functioned in separate worlds in Europe, but in America things were to be different. For one thing, their limited numbers made intermarriage inevitable; and for another, their business interests brought them together. And now that they were Americans, their outlook on life and the religion that had been basically unchanged since

Biblical times began to evolve into something quite different than what their forefathers knew.

Their faith had held the Jews together for thousands of years, but it had also set them apart from the secular world around them. In Europe after the Middle Ages, they had retreated into their own self-contained communities, often by force, and had governed themselves under the laws of the Talmud. In most cases, the civil authorities were just as happy to let the rabbis deal with their own problems as long as they followed the general rules of the larger community, stayed apart and paid their taxes. But when the first Jews began arriving in America, they didn't have rabbis in their midst, and were forced to rely on communities abroad to interpret religious law. In the meantime, none of the American colonies made any moves to set them apart, and the laymen who ran the synagogues were more than happy to let the individuals in their congregations be governed by the civil authorities.

By the time the American Constitution was ratified, the Jews had become such an integral part of the larger society that some of its leaders were beginning to worry that they had lost their traditional identity. Most, in fact, identified with the German community. It was only natural, the majority had come to America in the great German migration of the mid-nineteenth century. Most of them had been tradesmen there, and as Americans, most supported themselves as peddlers. New arrivals tended to settle in cities, where they found the competition fierce. But they found a need in the countryside, and began carrying merchandise on their backs into rural areas. Eventually, they expanded their business by investing in horse carts and it was only a matter of time before they began establishing dry goods stores in small towns, where they were more than welcome. Family groups provided the necessary credit, and some became wholesalers. The Jewish community also filled its own need for bookkeepers, as well as the factory workers who produced the goods other members of the community offered for sale. In time, there wasn't a city anywhere in the country that didn't have at least a small Jewish community. And wherever they settled, they adapted to the needs of their neighbors, branching out from retailing to banking and, especially in the far West, they became active in civic affairs. For them, it was a very untraditional thing to do, but America was changing their traditional outlook on life. By the 1840s, the Jews were beginning to make changes in the religion itself. They still wanted to keep the old teachings, but they wanted to be taught in English and not German or Hebrew. The first rabbis began arriving at about the same time and they were by and large young Germans who had been involved in the movement to reform the religious life of the Jews. They were interested in sweeping away the archaic laws and ceremonies that they felt only separated them from society, and making the religion more sensitive to the things Jews had in common with the Gentiles rather than the things that kept them apart. Their ideas were considered radical, even dangerous, in Europe. But in America, the reform movement was met with open arms.

It allowed them to integrate even more thoroughly into American life, and in the years just before the Civil War, the sons of peddlers were among the wealthiest bankers and retailers in the country's biggest cities. At the time, there were about two hundred fifty Jews in America, and nearly all of them traced their roots to Germany and nearby Poland. By the beginning of World War I, there were four million Jews in America, and most had emigrated from Eastern Europe.

The so-called Russian Jews didn't follow the established pattern of settlement, but stayed in the larger cities, especially New York, where they represented almost forty-five percent of the city's population in 1920. They lived in cramped ghettos where they formed tight communities not a lot different from the social structure they had left behind: But America worked its magic on them, too. In the Old World, the rabbis had regulated their lives, here the religious leaders were forced to bow to outside civil authority. They could perform marriages, but it was illegal for them to grant divorces, for instance. At the same time, the immigrants couldn't afford to pay a rabbi, and many congregations decided it was acceptable to be without one. The job of educating their children fell to the state rather than the religious community as had been a traditional part of Orthodox Jewish life. Parents were anxious to see their children succeed in the new country, and encouraged them in getting a secular education, something that had been unthinkable to their own parents. In the process, Orthodoxy went through a process of Americanization, and as its adherents became Americanized, too, they began leaving the ghetto. They brought the traditions out with them, but with some new ideas that were alien to the world they left behind.

They also brought out a new enthusiasm for socialism and Zionism, which eventually bound all American Jews together and changed some American institutions in the bargain. Around the turn of the century, their ideas put them at the center the trade union movement, which changed conditions not only for Jews but for everyone who worked for a living.

Organizing labor in America had been an uphill battle for generations, but at the end of 1909, Jewish and Italian girls who worked in clothing sweatshops organized a four-month strike and managed to hold out against antagonistic police and judges, not to mention management goon squads that threatened their lives. They found help among Jewish socialist feminists and Jewish philanthropic organizations. A few months later, the cloak makers called a similar strike, and once again influential Jews came to their aid and forced a settlement favorable to the workers. Ironically, management was largely Jewish, too, and the warfare between them and their workers spawned a movement among the German Jews, who had stayed aloof of their Russian counterparts, to offer more help to the newcomers on the theory that dissension within the Jewish community was a bad reflection on the community as a whole. Their Jewishness was all they had in common, but it had held them together for thousands of years, after all. And it was that sense of community that gave organized labor its first real toehold in the United States.

At the same time, second and third generation American Jews who had never experienced any form of discrimination began finding it lurking around every corner. But though they had entertained thoughts of distancing themselves from the new immigrants, they accepted the responsibility of helping them assimilate into American society. As they became identified with each other in the eyes of their Gentile neighbors, they began to debate the pros and cons of whether America's strength comes from its cultural diversity or or whether it is truly a great melting pot creating an entirely new race. The jury is still out. But at this moment in American history, we celebrate our differences with all the enthusiasm we can muster. On the other hand, the melting pot is still bubbling. On March 17, we all wear green and ask each other, "did your mother come from Ireland?" We celebrate Columbus Day, not in honor of the discovery of America, but as the contribution of an Italian in the service of a Spanish king. People of every race mark the birthday of Dr. Martin Luther King Jr., and when the Germans turn out to remember Baron von Steuben, we raise a glass of beer to his memory without giving a single thought that he was a hero of the American Revolution who happened to have been German. And when we go out for dinner, chances are it won't be to an American restaurant. Maybe tonight we feel like Chinese food, or Italian or French. Even McDonald's has added pizza to its menu.

For all our diversity, though, America is the sum of its parts, and if you were to be taken blindfolded to a strange city in any part of the country, it would probably take a while to figure out where you were. Consider the case of Erwin Kreuz. A few years back, Erwin, a brewery worker from West Germany, got off a plane in Bangor, Maine, and strolled into the terminal building to sample the local beer, which he found acceptable. He then set out to see the sights. He was impressed, and why not? Bangor is a terrific place to visit, and Erwin drank it in for three days. But all the while he had the feeling that something was wrong. He thought he was in San Francisco. But he couldn't find a cable car, and though he was sure it was out there somewhere, the Golden Gate Bridge wasn't looming on the horizon as he thought it should be. He found a Chinese restaurant, but no Chinatown. There were no skyscrapers, either, and the hills didn't seem worth writing home about. Finally someone broke the news to him that all those things were three thousand miles away. But the State O'Mainers invited him to stay a few more days, then they packed him aboard a westbound plane and he got to see San Francisco after all. In some ways, it looked a lot like Bangor. Same supermarkets, same fast food restaurants, same television programs. It didn't have the same abundance of lobsters, but the local crabs are just as good and, as Erwin found out for himself, so is the beer.

His adventure is almost the story of America. Back in 1492, Christopher Columbus discovered it , but he was so sure he was someplace else, he called the natives "Indians." Columbus was out to prove that the world was round, and he was certain he could reach the exotic East by sailing west. When he realized he wasn't in India, he moved on.

About five-hundred years before him, Norsemen led by Leif Ericson apparently stumbled on North America. They called it "Vineland the Good," but didn't think it was good enough to either to stay or to make a record of their discovery. There are stories that Swedes and Norwegians came to America from Greenland in the thirteenth century. And still others say that America was discovered by the Irish, or the Welsh, or the Chinese or the Phoenicians. But through it all, none of them seems to have known what they discovered. And none of them seems to have cared.

Once it had been officially discovered, though, people began coming to explore it. But in almost every case, what they were really looking for was a way around it or through it. Columbus never knew he had discovered a whole new continent, but he found out enough about it to know that it was rich in gold and silver; and to the Spanish who financed his trips, that was a whole lot better than spices from the Orient or some half-baked theory about the shape of the world. Within twenty years, they were exporting a million dollars a year in gold and silver from their American possessions, and that encouraged them to look around for more.

In the process, they established colonies, including St. Augustine on the Florida peninsula. It was the first permanent European settlement in what is now the United States. It was so permanent, in fact, that it's still there. Meanwhile, watching Spain's wealth grow encouraged others to have a look around on their own. French explorers claimed all the territory north from the Carolinas to the St. Lawrence River, and settled in Florida, South Carolina and Nova Scotia. The English got into the act, too, but they found it more fun to raid Spanish treasure ships than to build towns and farms. One of the pirates, Sir Walter Raleigh, used his Spanish treasure to start a colony in Virginia. It ultimately failed, but not before it introduced tobacco to a breathlessly-waiting world and made British merchants realize there was, perhaps, more to America than gold and silver.

Europeans began arriving and seriously settling down in the seventeenth century. The English set up shop in Jamestown, Virginia in 1607, and a year later, the French arrived in Quebec. Twenty years later, the Dutch established a business enterprise they called Nieuw Amsterdam, and ten years after that, the Swedes established a colony in Delaware. The Dutch eased them out rather quickly, but they were soon eased out themselves by the British who changed the name of the colony to New York.

While all this was going on, the French were pushing inland toward the Great Lakes and down the Mississippi River toward the Gulf of Mexico. The stage was set for war.

There were four wars in all, beginning with the one called King William's War, and ending with the Seven Years' War. Oddly enough, none was fought in America, but America was what they were all about. When they were over, France had lost her claim to her American colonies, and England and Spain divided the continent between them. It was a simple arrangement, the Spanish got all the territory west of the Mississippi, and the English controlled everything east of the river.

The Spanish thought they had made a good deal. They had found great riches among the Aztecs and Incas in Central and South America, and the Indians had told them there were seven cities of gold not far to the north. Indeed, a Spanish priest in search of heathen to convert, reported having seen one of them somewhere near the present-day Arizona-New Mexico border. The Conquistadores had been exploring the territory for a century, going as far north as Kansas and west into California. They never did find the fabled seven golden cities, but they were convinced they couldn't possibly be east of the Mississippi.

The British were slow starters in colonizing America, but they were the most successful. In 1620, just a few years after the founding of the Virginia colony, a group of religious dissenters arrived in Cape Cod Bay, Massachusetts. As Puritans, life in England under King James I had been less than joyous, even to these people who considered "joy" a four-letter word, so there was no question of ever going back, no matter what life in America might turn out to be. Their ship, of course, was the Mayflower , their colony Plymouth, and they are remembered today as our "Pilgrim Fathers." They were Englishmen first and foremost, traveling with the permission of the Crown, and at the expense of the London Company, which owned the colony in Virginia.

Some say they were blown off course, some say it was a careful plan. But the fact is they landed far north of Virginia, just outside the jurisdiction of the London Company. That left them free to make their own rules, and before leaving the ship, they drew up a document that became the law of their new colony. Basically, it bound them together to voluntarily obey the rule of the majority. It was a revolutionary idea in 1620, but it planted the seeds of democracy in the New World and was the first step toward an even more revolutionary document, the United States Constitution.

Life was far from easy for the colonists on Cape Cod Bay, but they managed to survive. Within thirty years they had been joined by more than 20,000 hard-working souls in the biggest mass migration England had ever seen, and in the process they had seen the establishment of new towns with names like Boston and Cambridge, Charlestown and Gloucester. As often happens when oppressed people look for freedom, the Massachusetts settlers didn't give much freedom to people who didn't agree with them. It wasn't long before they had dissenters in their midst, who went down the Cape to Narragansett Bay and established a new colony called Rhode Island. The soil in Massachusetts was poor for farming, so another group moved south and settled down along the Connecticut River, which made the Dutch in nearby Nieuw Amsterdam very nervous, indeed. More of them moved "down east" into Maine, which had already been settled by the French, and still more moved west into New Hampshire.

The Indians had been friendly, even helpful, to the colonists, but all this expansion was more than they could bear. The Puritans didn't believe in buying territory from the natives, they just marched in and took it. The tribes in Connecticut didn't think much of that idea and rebelled by attacking the new settlements. In retaliation, a small army was sent out from Massachusetts and wiped out an entire tribe, destroying their villages and capturing the survivors to sell as slaves in the West Indies. That solved the settlers' immediate problem, but it gave them a much bigger one in return. And so to protect themselves from the Indians, who had suddenly turned hostile to everyone's surprise, they formed a confederation they called "New England."

Meanwhile, people were pouring into the New World from old England. The king was giving away huge tracts of land to his cronies and his creditors. Among them was his old friend Sir George Calvert, who had been banished from Virginia because he was a Catholic. The grant eventually went to Calvert's son, the second Lord Baltimore, who named his new territory Maryland, and established a colony for English Catholics.

One of the men who received a royal gift of American territory was interested in religious freedom for Quakers who were being persecuted not only in England and Ireland but in America as well. But William Penn didn't draw the line at Quakers. His colony welcomed anyone, with the result that colonial Pennsylvania was the fastest-growing of all the English settlements in America. They came from Ireland, Wales and

Scotland as well as from Sweden and Germany, and they all agreed they liked what they found in Mr. Penn's colony. Even the natives were friendly. Penn was fair-minded to a fault, and made it a point to pay the Indians for the land the king had given to him. He also negotiated treaties that were fair to both sides, and made sure they were honored. The result was that Pennsylvania farmers, who didn't bother to own guns, lived in complete peace with the Indians while settlers all around them lived in terror of the "savages."

More than fifty years passed before the last of the English colonies was established on the Eastern Seaboard when James Oglethorpe established Georgia as a haven for people in English debtors' prisons. During those decades, cities grew, trappers and farmers began moving inland and immigrants poured in from all over Europe. By 1760, the population had soared to 1.7 million, the country was prosperous and the cities cosmopolitan. A whole continent stretched out to the west waiting to be conquered. But first something had to be done about the British.

It started quietly at first. Most wars do. Word had gone out that the British were on the way to Lexington, Massachusetts to arrest a pair of rebels named John Hancock and Sam Adams. About seventy patriots, who called themselves "Minutemen," assembled to take a stand against them. And there, on April 19, 1775, a pistol shot rang out, followed by a volley of rifle fire and men fell dead. Within a month Great Britain was at war with her American colonies. It would last until 1781 when General George Washington, with the help of the French Marquis de Lafayette, defeated the Red Coats at Yorktown, Virginia. As the British marched away, their band played an old march, "The World Turned Upside Down." And for them it had. America was finally a free and independent nation. Thirteen colonies had united against the Mother Country, and their new country covered eight hundred thousand square miles from Maine to Georgia and from the Atlantic Ocean to the Mississippi River. Today, the fifty United States cover more than 3.6 million square miles, and the population has grown from about three million in 1781 to 244.6 million today.

And still the debate goes on about what a "typical" American might be. From the point of view of census statistics, the average American family would seem to live in a metropolitan suburb at about the point where Wyoming, Montana and South Dakota come together. Since there are no large cities anywhere near there, one can't help being cynical about statistical evidence. But to press on ... the typical American family, say the demographers, owns its own home, which is worth about $17,000 (in a metropolitan suburb, mind you). The family is is about ninety percent white, but speaks a little Spanish, looks slightly Oriental and had ancestors who were pure American Indians. The man of the house is forty-four years old and his wife admits to being about forty-one. They have 3.5 children, whom they support on an annual income of $9,867. But they are still affluent enough to own one and a quarter automobiles.

And so on. Every American family appears to own three radios, and more Americans own a TV set than have a bathtub or a shower in their house. They're religious, too. Only about five percent say they have no religion at all. And of the rest sixty-six percent are Protestant, twenty-six percent are Catholic and three percent are Jewish. The other five percent are divided among nearly all the religions known to mankind.

The politicians are fond of wringing their hands over the thousands they say "go to bed hungry every night," but an overwhelming percentage of Americans are on diets, and the average American family spends more on food alone than the total income of the average Greek family.

We're also, it seems, a nation of movers. The statisticians tell us that some twenty percent of American families look for greener pastures every year, and sometimes the moving amounts to a mass migration. Incredible numbers have moved from the South to the North in the last half-century, and almost as many have gone the other way. Farm workers have gone to the cities, and city-dwellers to the suburbs, and California never

seems to stop growing. But the more the people move around, the more the population centers stay the same. Less than two percent of the land is taken up by cities, and more than half of all Americans live close enough to plan a Sunday picnic on the shores of the Atlantic or Pacific Oceans, the Gulf of Mexico or one of the Great Lakes. And though only about a quarter of all native-born Americans are living in the state where they were born, more than a quarter of the total population is crowded along the Eastern Seaboard, about the same percentage that lived there a century ago.

But in the years since the Revolution, the pull has been from the West. When the war ended, the Spanish still controlled Florida and all that territory west of the Mississippi. The defeated British had never bothered to go home from Ohio, and just about everything west of the original thirteen colonies was wilderness occupied by trappers and traders, Indians and a few farmers. A generation later, the United States bought a piece of the former Spanish territory that the French had annexed and called "Louisiana," a vast territory that began at the Mississippi, went past Texas and stretched west through present-day Montana and Wyoming and on into the Pacific Northwest. It doubled the size of the country and provided a new incentive to move west.

People began taking advantage of the opportunities in the 1820s when the waves of immigrants began arriving from Europe, eager for a new life and willing to take a chance on the wild frontier. People who had been born in places like Connecticut and Maryland joined them, lured by the promise of cheap land. Farmers from the already soil-exhausted South picked up stakes and went along, too. Others went in search of adventure, and some to escape debt. But most went west just because it was there. It gave them a chance to start a new life, something Americans are still doing almost 170 years later.

By the time the migration to the West got really serious, there were passable roads across the Appalachian Mountains. The migrants went in Conestoga wagons, in pack trains, in fancy stagecoaches. Once across the mountains, the Ohio River took them into Tennessee and Kentucky ... all the way to the Mississippi, in fact. From there it was relatively easy to get to the Great Lakes, the Gulf of Mexico and across into Missouri and Arkansas.

Their new homes were in hostile wilderness, populated by Indians who didn't much like seeing their hunting grounds turned into farms, and by French and British agitators who egged the savages on. But those who ventured into Ohio found signs of a very friendly man whose mission in life was to make their lives pleasanter.

His name was John Chapman. When he died in the 1830s, the Fort Wayne, Indiana, Sentinel reported:

> Died in the neighborhood of this city on Tuesday last, Mr. John Chapman,
> better-known as Johnny Appleseed. The deceased was well-known throughout
> this region by his eccentricity, and the strange garb he usually wore. He
> followed the occupation of nursery-man.

Remembering Johnny Appleseed as a "nursery-man" is like remembering George Washington as a "planter." Chapman wandered through the wilderness for more than fifty years planting apple trees and other fruits and medicinal plants he knew would be useful to the settlers who followed.

He began his wanderings in Pittsburgh after having planted orchards all the way from Massachusetts to Pennsylvania. Everyone who knew him loved him, even the Indians, who were generally hostile to white men. But even those who admired him had to admit that he cut quite a bizarre figure. They said his shirt was an old coffee sack with armholes ripped out and that a stewing kettle passed for a hat. At the end of most days, he would appear at the door of a settler's cabin asking for shelter for the night. When he was welcomed inside, he always refused to sleep anywhere but on the bare floor and before the sun rose in the morning he had vanished as mysteriously as he appeared.

Once, when the city of Mansfield, Ohio, was being attacked by Indians, Chapman ran thirty miles to the nearest fort and was back again with help in less than twenty-four hours. Another story about him, which may or may not be true, was that he was seen in the woods playing with a family of bear cubs while their mother benignly looked on. He always walked barefoot, even in winter, and they said he could find his way anywhere without a compass.

Deeply religious, Johnny led an utterly selfless life. He didn't own a gun, and couldn't hurt any living thing. A legend about him says that he once doused a campfire so the mosquitoes wouldn't be burned to death. He refused to eat meat, and would never accept anything from anyone unless he could exchange it for some seeds or a small tree.

When Ohio began to get too crowded for him, he moved west into Indiana where he finally died. For years after people on the frontier told affectionate stories about this wonderful little man. There were so many stories, in fact, that people who didn't know better began to think there never had been such a person as Johnny Appleseed. But if he was too good to be true, he did exist, and he was a sign of hope for the people who were building a new country.

By the time he died, there were more than a million people living in Ohio and three million more living in other places west of the Allegheny Mountains. It was about then that President James Monroe decided it was time to do something about all those Indians who stood in the way of expansion. General Andrew Jackson and Indiana's Governor, William Henry Harrison, both future presidents, rose to the challenge and defused the Indian menace and established a standing army to keep them in their place. But the government decided that their place was elsewhere. New treaties dictated that the eastern tribes should move into the West ahead of the white emigrants. The Creeks, Cherokees, Choctaws, Chickasaws and Seminoles were all forced to walk what they called the "Trail of Tears" into what the Government called "Indian Territory."

They called it "progress." It's a thing Americans still believe in with unabashed enthusiasm. No problem is so great that "American Ingenuity" can't solve it. America first discovered its courage, and its ingenuity, through the people who moved west in the early nineteenth century. They took civilization into the wilderness and made it work. Long before the century was over, the country was well on its way, not just to the Pacific coast, but to a status in the world no country so young had any right to expect.

One of the people who originally explored the land just west of the mountains fired the imagination of all would-be frontiersmen and still inspires us today. His name was Daniel Boone, a Pennsylvanian who grew up in North Carolina and spent most of his life exploring Kentucky. On his first trip into the interior, he was captured and robbed by Indians four times and after four years of hunting came back empty-handed. But he loved every minute of it and he became a master of Indian psychology as well as an enthusiastic hunter and explorer.

He was also a master story-teller, and his tales of the wilderness encouraged a North Carolina entrepreneur to buy all of Kentucky and part of Tennessee from the Cherokees. His yarns also landed him the job of mapping the new acquisition. Once into the interior, he built a town which he modestly named "Boonesboro." But he had no sooner taken up residence than he was taken prisoner by the Shawnee Indians, who hadn't been in on the deal with the Cherokees and decided to destroy the town and get rid of the settlers. But Boone talked them out of their plan and in the process so charmed them that they adopted him into their tribe, with the new name "Big Turtle," and treated him like the son of their chief. But all the while, Daniel Boone was still their prisoner.

Several months passed before he was able to escape, and he got back to Boonesboro just in time to warn the town that the Indians were on their way. By the time the attack began, the settlers were ready and determined to fight to the death to save their homes. They very nearly had to. The Shawnee kept up their siege for two months, trying every trick in the book to destroy the place. But Daniel Boone had learned all their tricks, and so none of them worked. Finally, the Shawnee tried digging a tunnel to get under the stockade, but Boone countered by digging a trench in their way. They kept at it anyway, until a heavy downpour collapsed their tunnel and they decided that, too, must have been the work of the Big Turtle. They went home in disgust and never came near Boonesboro again.

He had saved his home, but Daniel Boone had never been a homebody. Leaving the great Wilderness Road as a permanent monument, he set out to explore even more of the country. At the age of sixty-five, when most people today think of retirement, he joined the Lewis and Clark Expedition up the Missouri River and into the Oregon Territory.

He opened the way for people as tough as himself. Men and women with large numbers of children built log cabins in the middle of the wilderness and went to work to carve out new lives. They usually cleared about forty acres by stripping the bark from the trees so that they would die. Once dead, all they had to do was burn away the trunks, dig up the stumps and when they were finished, they had farmland where a forest once stood. In places where there were no trees, they burned the tall grass so new grass would feed their cattle. It was all backbreaking, time consuming work relegated to the men and boys. Women and girls looked after the younger children when they weren't cooking, churning, hoeing, spinning, chopping wood or carrying water.

Not everyone lived in the wilderness, though. Great cities were being established, too. Cincinnati, Pittsburgh and Detroit were all lusty and thriving by the beginning of the nineteenth century, and in a 1795 treaty the Indians had turned over "a piece of land six miles square at the mouth of the Chickago River, emptying into the southwest end of Lake Michigan where a fort formerly stood." In 1803 a new fort was built there to stand guard over the gateway to the Northwest Territory. Some French traders, holdovers from the days when it was French territory, lived across the river, but it was a quiet place that didn't seem to have much of a future.

The fort was destroyed during the War of 1812 and rebuilt soon after. It became the center of the fur trade for a while, but eventually the trappers went elsewhere. The problem was that they had to carry their canoes across a portage at that point and they decided to look for an easier place to do business. Then someone had the bright idea of replacing the portage with a canal and the City of Chicago was born.

New York City has an international flavor that can't be matched by any other city in the world; San Francisco has a classic charm that makes it the favorite city of most Americans; Denver has a setting that makes it the envy of most other cities, but no other city on the North American continent is quite as "American" as Chicago, Illinois. New York, Boston and Philadelphia were all well into their second century when people began settling along the lake shore. But this city was different. For the first time, possibly in the history of the world, builders asked women what sort of houses they'd like. The answer was loud and clear. They wanted porches and big bay windows and yards that went around all four sides of the house. They got what they wanted. Chicago was a neighborly place then, and it still is.

It is where modern architecture was born and where it exists at its best. It is the city of Frank Lloyd Wright and Mies van der Rohe and the man who started it all, Louis Sullivan. Sullivan's philosophy was based on the tradition of early builders talking with the people who had to use their buildings. He didn't think a bank should look like a fortress or a factory like a tomb. His ideas were taken abroad and sent back as "international style." But as cities like Atlanta and Dallas seem to prove, the Sullivan philosophy that "a building is an act" got lost somewhere in the translation.

The good news is that Chicago is alive and well. Anyone searching for America would do well to start there. In its early days, once the frontier had pushed that far west, it became the Gateway to the Golden West. But the gate swung both ways. It also became the gateway to the East and South for the ranchers and farmers in the West, and by the beginning of the Civil War, Chicago was already what Carl Sandburg later called "Hog butcher for the world." As the railroads pushed west, Chicago was at the center of the excitement. It still has the biggest railroad station in the world and the busiest airport, and it's still the Gateway to the Golden West.

The territory north of Chicago – Wisconsin, Michigan, Minnesota and all the way west to Oregon – was a land of logging camps in the early days. Instead of burning out the forests as the farmers had done in the South and East, they were at work providing the raw material to build a new country. The loggers in the Northwest, the keelboatmen on the Mississippi, the farmers and builders were all made of tough stuff. There was hard work to be done, and they were the right people for the job. Hard work had been an American tradition right from the start, and they made it look easy.

When Indiana was still at the edge of the frontier, the territory between the Missouri River and the Spanish missions in California was wild, hostile, unexplored country. It was a perfect setting for the rugged individualists who called themselves Mountain Men. It was all the rage in London and Paris in the 1820s to have soft felt hats made of beaver fur. They were as expensive as they were fashionable, and beaver pelts brought good prices. Trappers who thought the profits were worth the risk armed themselves with big rifles, tomahawks and hunting knives and ran their trap lines across the plains and into the Rocky Mountains beyond. Some years later, Buffalo Bill made himself the personification of these first white men to see the great buffalo herds on the plains, the first to ride through the Rockies, and the first to fight the Apache and other fierce Indian tribes in the West. They wore big-brimmed hats and fringed leather jackets and trousers; their faces were smeared with campfire grease and their long matted hair streamed out behind them as they rode over trails only Indians had even seen.

They lived their lives in the mountains and on the prairies, slipping back toward the East once a year to meet traders out from St. Louis to exchange beaver pelts for whiskey and fresh clothes.

Meanwhile, the Spanish hadn't given up looking for those fabled seven cities of gold, but by then they had confined their search to the Southwest from Texas and New Mexico and into California. They had missions and settlements along the California coast from San Diego to San Francisco. But the Americans were beginning to talk about "Manifest Destiny," a belief that God had sent them to fill up the continent; the Indians in the desert were getting weary of Spanish soldiers and missionaries roaming over their territory, and to make matters even worse, the Russians were coming.

The czar was as interested as anyone else to find a Northwest Passage across the American continent and he sent an explorer named Vitus Bering to have a look. Bering explored Alaska and discovered it was rich with otter, a happy little animal whose fur was highly-prized in China. The information lured trappers from Siberia who began establishing settlements along the coast almost as far south as the Spanish mission at San Francisco. At the same time, British fur traders had moved west across Canada. And Americans, including John Jacob Astor, a New Yorker who had emigrated from Germany, began setting up trading posts at the edge of the Oregon Territory. The days of Spanish California were clearly numbered.

Back East, Americans had begun dreaming a new dream. Until then, the lure of the West had been gold or timber or furs. But the new dream was for the land itself. Most of the immigrants from Europe had come from peasant stock and the idea of actually owning their own land was almost too incredible to contemplate. The idea of going to the West where land was available and cheap took the country by storm.

The major trails began at Independence, Missouri, the jumping-off place for the Santa Fe Trail into the Southwest, and the Oregon Trail that headed north toward the Columbia River. It was a boom town in the 1840s, with pioneers arriving by the hundreds with their families and all their belongings loaded into canvas-covered ox-drawn wagons. They usually stayed at Independence for a several weeks, buying new supplies, hiring guides and organizing themselves into trains of about forty wagons each.

Once underway on the Oregon Trail, they found the countryside beautiful, the prairie carpeted with wildflowers and the sky as wide and blue as any they had ever seen in their lives. But it was ominously quiet out there. The only break in the silence was an occasional violent rainstorm that washed out their camps and flooded the streams often in a matter of minutes. But they were ready for that, their wagons were built to double as boats. They were ready for almost anything, in fact. The wagons moved four abreast so they could quickly be formed into squares in the event of a sudden Indian attack, and the men leading the oxen kept a sharp lookout. The boys brought up the rear, keeping the cattle from straying and the women sat in the wagons, usually knitting. It was a bumpy ride, but for the first few weeks, at least, it was almost fun. They were on their way to a new life, they were forming new friendships and it looked like their new world was going to be a wonderful place.

Their relative boredom came to an abrupt end when they reached Chimney Rock in western Nebraska and their wagon wheels began to sink into the sandy soil. They were usually out of firewood by then, but there were no trees to cut and they were forced to cook over buffalo chip fires. Their next landmark, Fort Laramie, Wyoming, gave them a chance to load fresh supplies, to rest their livestock and get up the courage to face the real challenge just ahead in the distance, the Rocky Mountains.

The trail across Wyoming toward Idaho was littered with cast-off furniture, abandoned to make loads lighter for starving oxen. It was uphill all the way until they came to a pass that took them across the top of the mountains, and their first look at even more hostile country stretching out ahead of them. If they were lucky enough to make it before winter, they settled down in Oregon and California, and they never looked back. Yet, oddly, even native Californians today refer to anything on the other side of the Mississippi River as "back East."

The Oregon Trail, which has since been paved as Interstate Route 80, was laid out by the Lewis and Clark Expedition; the Santa Fe Trail was the route of mule trains and ox carts that carried American trade into New Mexico. It stretched almost eight hundred miles across the desert and through the homeland of the hostile Apache, so it wasn't nearly as popular with the early emigrants until gold fever hit them in 1849. People starting heading west for an entirely different reason, and would put up with almost any hardship to get there in a hurry.

A third route to the West figuratively began at Palmyra, New York, on the banks of the Erie Canal. A man named Joseph Smith was plowing his field there one day when, he said, an angel who called himself Moroni introduced him to God and His Son. Smith wrote a book about what they told him, which he called "The Book of Mormon," and started a whole new religion. Some of his neighbors in Palmyra didn't like the idea and ran Smith and his followers out of town. They had the same experience in Ohio and then again in Missouri, but even as they kept moving, the number of Smith's followers kept growing. They finally settled along the Mississippi in Illinois at a town they called Nauvoo. Before long, it was the biggest city in the state, bigger even than Chicago, with some fifteen thousand residents, and the Mormons thought they were safe at last. But they weren't. Nauvoo was surrounded by "Gentiles," as Smith called non-Mormons, who weren't too neighborly or tolerant of these people who practiced polygamy. When Smith ordered the destruction of a newspaper that had been critical of him, the Gentiles made their move. They lynched him.

Brigham Young replaced Smith as the leader of the flock and took on the mission of leading them to a land where there would be no Gentiles. They sold their houses and began building wagons that would take them to the Great Salt Lake, which had been discovered by Mountain Men whose descriptions made it seem just the kind of place the Mormons were looking for. A few of them had oxen to pull their wagons, but most loaded their belongings into handcarts and began walking across the plains. By the fall of 1847, some two thousand of them had made it to their Promised Land, but what they found there was a dry, sunken plain, not the Garden of Eden they had been told was there. But if faith can move mountains, it can make deserts bloom, too. They put themselves completely in the hands of their leaders and together they accomplished the transformation. Meanwhile, thousands of converts arrived from the East and Europe, and a string of settlements sprang up. Soon there were enough of them that Brigham Young felt justified in declaring that the Mormons had established a new nation that would henceforth be known as Deseret. The United States government had already staked its claim on the territory, though, and were just as intent to call it Utah. It took them nearly fifty years to make the idea stick.

Even the Civil War didn't slow the rush to the West. In the same year General Sherman marched across Georgia, some seventy-five thousand people marched in wagon trains along the Oregon Trail. And after the war ended in 1865, freed slaves and war veterans poured across the Mississippi looking for adventure and opportunity. What they found there was what they themselves created, the Wild West.

Most of the big cattle spreads were in Texas and Colorado, but the Texas ranchers drove their stock as far north as the Dakota Territory to fatten them up over the winter before shipping them east to Chicago. The cowboys who drove them a thousand miles north were a lusty lot who typically spent sixteen hours a day in the saddle, choking on dust, kept an eye peeled for marauding Indians, heading off stampedes and fighting rustlers and armed farmers who didn't like all those steers trampling their crops.

A trail drive included about twenty-five hundred head of cattle that were driven an average of fifteen hundred miles. A trail boss, in charge of about a dozen cowboys and a cook, was completely responsible for the whole operation and shared the profits once the cattle were sold. His cowhands were paid about thirty dollars a month, plus board. Naturally, all that work made a man thirsty, and the cow towns along their route obliged them with plenty to drink as well as friendly games of chance to help boost their income, and companionship to boost their morale. It was a tough life, often a short one, but to be a cowboy in the Wild West is still an American boy's fondest dream.

Cowboys, gunslingers and U.S. Marshals were only a small part of the population that tamed the West. In 1862, President Lincoln signed a law that entitled any American (or anyone who intended to become one) to 160 acres of land for nothing more than a small filing fee and a promise to live there and farm it for at least five years. Civil War veterans went by the thousands into Kansas and Nebraska, the Dakotas and Montana to take the government up on its offer. Newly-arrived Europeans were lured by the promise of a free farm, too, and in less than a generation, the country's population doubled. The cowboys called the newcomers "sodbusters." The law required them to be farmers, but the farms and their fences got in the way of cattle drives. The Indians weren't too pleased with all those miles of barbed wire, either, but it was clear to everyone that they were there to stay.

In yet another scheme to encourage settlement of the West, the government gave millions of acres of land to the railroads. They, in turn, mounted an advertising blitz telling Easterners "You Need a Farm," and thousands agreed. They carried their campaign into Europe, too, and Germans, Norwegians, Dutch, Swedes and Danes responded enthusiastically. In Minnesota and the Dakotas, the Scandinavian languages became as common as English and the accents are still there a century later. Those settlers arrived through New York, but unlike the earlier immigrants, they never saw the city. They were headed west, and the reception station on Ellis Island in New York Harbor included rail facilities in New Jersey that took them on the next leg of the journey without a long stopover. It was all very efficient, and it made the West more accessible than it had ever been.

So many people rushed into the West that the government decided it was time to move the Indians around again. They forced the Creeks and Seminoles to give up some of their land in the old Indian Territory, renamed it Oklahoma and on April 22, 1889, declared it open under the Homestead Act. Before the sun set that day almost two million acres

had been claimed and the cities of Guthrie and Oklahoma City were established. Four years later, the Government dispossessed the Cherokee and one hundred thousand people moved in on the first day it was open for white settlement.

Meanwhile, back East, the seaports were kept busy bringing in new people. Between 1855 and 1890, more than seven million immigrants arrived in the Port of New York alone, and they kept coming for another sixty years after that. Between 1890 and 1954, when the immigration laws were changed, more than twenty million people from just about every country in the world came to make their mark in America.

By 1872, it was apparent that all that expansion was dramatically changing the shape of the land. The Mountain Men wouldn't have recognized their lonely territory, and the old frontiers in Ohio and Tennessee were completely tamed. To preserve some of the original character of the land, the Government decided to set aside more than 3,470 square miles (an area bigger than the Commonwealth of Puerto Rico) in Wyoming, Montana and Idaho and call it Yellowstone National Park. It's the world's first national park, and still the biggest of the thirty-seven in America. It hasn't changed much since hunters, Indians and trappers roamed there two centuries ago, still a wild country with moose, elk and its famous population of bears. Its geothermal features include the Old Faithful Geyser, an American icon that ranks along with the Statue of Liberty as a symbol of America.

Yellowstone straddles the Continental Divide, a mountain range that separates the East from the West. Rivers to the east of it flow toward the Atlantic, and those on the other side empty into the Pacific Ocean. Further north in Montana, the Divide crosses over into Canada at Glacier National Park, home to bighorn sheep, grizzly bears and snow that never melts. It was named for the old glaciers that carved its breathtaking valleys and lakes, but there are still glaciers there and it's as much like Alaska as any spot in the lower forty-eight states.

Daniel Boone would still recognize the country's most-visited national park, the Great Smoky Mountains in North Carolina and Tennessee. He'd be familiar with the log cabins and split rail fences, and he'd probably stop for a chat with the blacksmith or pick up some corn meal at the grist mill. But he would be surprised to find nature trails for cars. Actually, though, if he thought about it, he'd probably smile at the thought that the majority of the eight million people who tour the Smokies every year almost never get out of their cars, leaving the mountaintops and winding trails as quiet and peaceful as they ever were – even though there are so many people nearby. It makes it possible to explore the landscape in the same way he did, and possibly not run into anyone else doing the same thing.

Americans are very attached to their cars and rarely go anywhere without them. The result is that many of us see America as a land of superhighways carefully designed to take us around the cities and towns, with interchanges filled with ugly gas stations, tacky motels and fast food stands. Others in search of America fly over it in big jets, hoping there are no clouds over the Grand Canyon to spoil the view.

It's a part of America that makes life convenient and allows us to get to places our grandfathers couldn't have dreamed of seeing. But there's another America out there, and it's worth exploring.

Way out West in the wilds of New Mexico, there's a roadside oasis that's a combination gas station, general store, meat market, restaurant and dance hall. On Friday nights, folks drop by for a little companionship, a little something to eat and a few beers. Some of them travel as far as a hundred miles for the pleasure, because people are few and far between out there. The population is 0.3 persons per square mile, in fact.

The Friday night get-togethers are repeated in dozens of places along the old cattle-driving trails. They were generally spaced about a day's drive apart and usually boasted as well. Today they pump gas rather than water and their customers usually arrive in pickup trucks rather than on horseback. But they bring the spirit of the West along with them. They come to buy all their gas and most of their groceries, and if they feel like a night on the town, they order up a T-bone steak and a salad. They buy toys for their kids and batteries for their trucks; they make phone calls because most of them haven't bothered to install a telephone at home. And if the Friday night party lasts too long, they can stay the night in the attached motel.

In one of them on a Friday night not too long ago, a woodcutter who said he worked from six in the morning until sundown, seven days a week, summed up what it's all about. "When you're working that hard, that late, that long, you sure do appreciate having a place like this to come and have a beer and relax," he said. And why does he work that hard, that late, that long? "Sometimes I hate to come in," he added. "It gets so pretty out there it hurts your eyes."

Up among the cornfields of the Midwest, the rhythm of life is a bit different. People live in small towns with populations of five or six hundred on tree-shaded streets that criss-cross the main road where the stores are located. In many of them, the supper hour is announced at six o'clock with a blast from the whistle on top of the firehouse. An hour later, some of the kids drift downtown for an ice cream cone. They hang around for a while, but soon are replaced by teenagers out for a Coke and some friendly talk. They arrive on motorbikes or in souped-up cars with the rear-ends high in the air and the radios turned even higher. When they get tired of the video games at the local drive-in, they drive up and down the quiet streets impressing the girls on the sidewalk by "peeling rubber" as they take off from the traffic light. It doesn't take long for them to get bored with all that fun, and they settle down for serious discussions about the local high school football team; about girls, if they're boys; about boys, if they're girls. By eleven, the town has shut down for the night, and the only sounds are made by crickets or a truck just passing through.

While their kids are enjoying themselves downtown, the adults are probably sitting out on the front porch, talking softly with a neighbor, listening to the sounds of the night, or complaining about all that racket those kids are making with their cars. Some nights they go downtown themselves. Down to the Elks or the Moose, or the American Legion clubhouse. In many of America's small towns, the fraternal organizations are at the center of the social life. They promote Americanism, the old values, neighborliness. And they provide a place to have a friendly drink and good conversation. They might provide bingo games for the ladies, poker nights for their husbands and buffet dinners for the whole family. Sometimes on Saturday nights they pull out all the stops and turn the lodge hall into a dance hall where folks can take a turn to the music of Glenn Miller or Lawrence Welk, or follow the instructions of the caller at a good old-fashioned square dance.

Down in Georgia and Alabama and other parts of the Old South, community life is often centered around the churches. One of the lures of the fraternal organizations has always been in providing a place for an upstanding businessman to enjoy an occasional stinger or grasshopper without running the risk of offending customers who might see him leaving the local saloon. But in many parts of the South, "temperance" is too treasured a virtue for businessmen or politicians to unwind anywhere except behind the closed doors of their own homes.

The Southern churches, usually Methodist or Baptist, claim to give them all the unwinding they might need, with singing, praying and uplifting preaching. Everybody goes to Sunday school as well as church, and a church supper is an event no one ever misses. Many have one every Sunday afternoon, and the ladies spend much of the week getting ready by making casseroles and cakes, puddings, fried chicken, ham and biscuits. When it all comes together, it's one of life's purest pleasures. On the other hand, these Southern Protestants deny themselves one of the things many other Americans consider one of life's basic pleasures, dancing. Not long ago, a preacher in Knoxville, Tennessee, explained it to his parish by telling them that "any man who says he can dance and keep his thoughts pure is less than a man or he is a liar!" The congregation, as they often do,

responded with a resounding chorus of "Amen."

Sometimes Americans seek their pleasure by traveling abroad. But in their hearts, they know home's best. A woman in Dubuque, Iowa explained, "It was wonderful to get back to the Old World charm of Dubuque. You know, the hills are very reminiscent of Switzerland. And, oh, our river! I've never seen anything, neither the Danube nor the Seine, that's as beautiful as the Mississippi."

A lot of them travel around the United States sharing the pleasure of other regions. They travel in mobile homes, in pickup trucks which sit precariously in the back and up over the roof, and they travel in cars. For those in cars who aren't hauling their own sleeping quarters, there are more than fifty-five thousand motels waiting to serve them. And the number is growing fast. A few years ago, Holiday Inns reported it was adding a new motel to the American landscape every seventy-two hours.

In quieter times when there were no interstate highways and cars couldn't go any faster than thirty miles an hour, people often stayed in strange towns as paying guests in private houses that called themselves "tourist homes." A lot of them still exist, and the accommodations, much less formal than the thousands of inns that lure weekenders in search of country-cute, usually include a homemade breakfast, not with other visitors, but with the family that lives there. They charge a lot less, too. A typical tourist home might be a big old Victorian house on a small town's main street, its yard studded with bright orange day lilies, the lawn shaded by stately trees. The proprietors are often a retired couple living otherwise on a Social Security pension, and you can usually find them enjoying the comfort of wicker rockers on the wide porch in front of the house. The rooms they set aside for their paying guests are scrupulously clean and simply furnished. The twin beds may have been bought as surplus from a local hospital, or they may be leftovers from the time the house was filled with children. It's a slice of life left over from the 1930s, and though many people claim to long for those times when life was slower and people friendlier, the blithely pass it all by on a super highway that looks exactly like the one that passes near their own homes. Meanwhile, the place they're looking for is just beyond the embankment the highway builders put there to hide it from them.

The old ways are still alive and well along the quieter side roads. They live in New England clambakes, Louisiana crawfish festivals, Oklahoma rodeos and Iowa tractor-pulling contests. Little League baseball and Sunday afternoon softball games bind us to each other as well as to the past. High school football, band concerts and senior proms give us a sense of community. And the beauty and abundance of the land itself gives us a sense of pride.

Express passenger trains don't roar across the plains as often as they once did. Former hillbillies have become urbanized after moving to "Deetroit City" from the mountains of West Virginia. And a lot of the old cotton fields down South are producing soybeans these days. But they still ride to the hounds in Virginia and on Maryland's Eastern Shore. They still play sweet Dixieland music in New Orleans. They still wade through snow drifts to take the sweet sugar from Vermont's maple trees. They still make bourbon the old-fashioned way from good Kentucky corn. And they still produce, and drink, more beer than any nation on earth.

Dodge City, Kansas, "the wickedest city in the world" in Bat Masterson's day, is a little bit bigger and a whole lot less wicked these days. It's a tidy, prosperous city, home to seventeen thousand people who make farm machinery and drum heads and fatten cattle on the way to market. They also run a thriving business catering to visitors who are dying to see the cemetery up on Boot Hill. The women among them are much more likely to be wearing blue jeans than calico these days, and none of the men feels obliged to carry a six-gun any more.

Blue jeans, like jazz and corn on the cob, are America's most visible gifts to the world. But more important is America's spirit and enthusiasm and a thing we call the American Dream. From the first day the first settler arrived here from Europe, we have been excited about the idea that in America anything is possible. You can start from nothing and still be somebody. You can control your own destiny, realize your wildest dream; or even be free not to be upwardly-mobile if that's what your dream happens to be all about.

Of course, Americans don't really have a patent on such dreams, but they come true so often we sometimes tend to get smug about them. Back in 1959, Soviet Premier Nikita Khruschev toured the United States from the United Nations in New York to a farm in Coon Rapids, Iowa, and on to Hollywood, the world's ultimate dream factory. When he arrived in movie company's president, Spiros Skouras. That evening at dinner, Skouras, one of the great movie czars, explained to his guest that he had originally arrived in the United States as a penniless immigrant from Greece. "Only in America," he boasted, "could a young man with such humble beginnings make it straight to the top." "I understand that very well," replied Khruschev, "my father was a coal miner in Soviet Georgia."

Putdowns notwithstanding, the American Dream seems to be working very well. At last count, more than half a million Americans reported a net worth of more than a million dollars. Most of them live in New York and California; and Texas, the fabled land of oil millionaires, ranks tenth after such unlikely states as Indiana, Idaho and Minnesota.

Every day hundreds more follow the dream by renouncing foreign princes and potentates in the naturalization oath that turns them into citizens of the United States of America. Once having taken the oath, nothing at all distinguishes them from all the other American citizens who, if they haven't made the pledge themselves, are descended from someone who did. The process takes about three hours, including a literacy test, which ninety-five percent of the applicants pass easily. The current crop of new citizens come from diverse places. The judges who administer the oaths are seeing more and more Oriental faces these days, but mixed with them are blacks from the Caribbean islands, emigres from the Soviet Union, and, of course, people from the same places that have been sending their tempest-tossed to America's Golden Door for more than three hundred years. Once they become Americans, they move on to places like Moscow, Pennsylvania; Cairo, Georgia; Baghdad, Arizona; or they might even find themselves in Paradise, Michigan. Some might go to Canton, Illinois, which was named for Canton, China, by its original settlers who believed that's where you'd come out if you dug a hole right through the center of the earth. Or they might move out to West Texas to share the experience with the cowboy who once said, "You can lie on your belly and see for miles. Of course, there ain't nothing to see, if there was you could see it for sure." These new Americans might send their children to a one-room school in Nebraska, and find an opportunity for a public-supported, low-cost college education in nearly every state in the Union. They could get a job in a monster shopping mall just about anywhere. They can do just about anything they want. Anything, that is, except to become President of the United States, a job restricted to the native-born. But their children might one day sit in the Oval Office, even their girl children. And that, above all, is what the American Dream is all about.

Lobstermen (left) still set their traps in the icy Maine waters, just as their ancestors did, except nowadays their boats are motorized.

Cadillac Mountain (above), in Acadia National Park, is the highest point on the Eastern seaboard. From it one can see almost all the way to the "Wild West."

Perhaps the most spectacular view from Acadia's Cadillac Mountain is to be seen looking east (below) into the dawn.

Pemaquid Point Light (facing page), near Damariscotta, has been marking the harbor entrance since 1827. Today it also houses an art gallery and the Fisherman's Museum.

State O' Mainers are known for the stories they tell down at the general store.

One of the famous stories you might have heard told in a Maine general store is the one about the year a dairy barn got snowbound in September and stayed that way until May.

Winter was not as much fun in New England before ski resorts, such as that at Waterville Valley, New Hampshire, were built.

Up in the New Hampshire hills (above), locals call fall visitors "leaf peepers." But you will never hear a peep of displeasure from either host or guest.

Traditional methods of furniture-making are still practiced in New Hampshire; some cribs (above) are still made the old-fashioned way.

Portsmouth, at one time New Hampshire's capital, was first settled in 1623 and ever since has carefully preserved its history. A visitor could be forgiven for thinking he had stepped back in time on encountering a Civil War reenactment (right).

At 6,288 feet tall, Mount Washington (above), is the principal peak in the Presidential Range of the White Mountains and the highest point in New England.

The valley at the foot of the Presidential Range contains dozens of ski resorts, such as Attitash Mountain Village (left).

It could be Scotland, but don't be fooled. It is really Lake Willoughby (right) in northeastern Vermont.

"There's always snow in Stowe," they say. But some of the time it is only to be found on the summit of Mount Mansfield (below).

The Rock of Ages Company operates several granite quarries (above) in Millstone Hill, Barre. Granite excavated here has supplied the materials for public buildings all over America, and provides the nation with a third of its memorial stones.

In the Manchester area, in the foothills of the Taconics and dominated by Mount Equinox, even the scarecrows (right) look friendly.

There are many ways to enjoy the snow – on skis or snowshoes or, perhaps most exhilarating, riding in crisp snow (below).

Hardy folk might hike along the shores of Lake Champlain, overlooked by the Adirondacks and the Green Mountains, but if you prefer a pew with a view, a "surrey with fringe on top" is the answer.

Picking the right horse at a harness race (above), in which the horses draw a sulky and driver, is one of the surest ways to enjoy a New England country fair.

A spectacular view unfolds beneath visitors taking a leisurely ride in a cable car over Mount Mansfield.

*The harvest is in, the silos
are filled, but there is still
plenty of work to be done
on the farm.*

Even during the hard
Vermont winters (left),
outdoor work continues
and the workers must be
supplied with food.

In the fall, wholesome
fresh cabbages and
plump squashes (above)
are enough to make you
wonder why in the world
you didn't like that stuff
when you were a kid.

Feeding the precious
young stock.

Making maple syrup
(right) can be hard work,
but the mouth-watering
result makes all the effort
seem worthwhile.

Even on a farm, there are
moments to sit on the
front steps (below) and
enjoy life.

Harvard University (left) spans the past and present with an evolution of buildings dating from as early as 1720 to as recently as 1989. Here the likes of Longfellow, Oliver Wendell Holmes and T.S. Eliot studied.

The Pilgrim Myles Standish, who explored the Cape in a small boat before the Pilgrims disembarked, would hardly recognize the landing point at Provincetown (below) on old Cape Cod.

The brig Beaver II (facing page), moored at Boston's Griffin's Wharf (facing page), is a Danish brig, first launched in 1908, which has been fitted out as a replica of one of the Tea Party ships – costumed forms are still to be seen tossing tea chests overboard.

Harvard University was established to train ministers, but now it offers students a wide range of activities including ballet (left) in its beautifully lit sports halls.

Outdoor sports are also taken very seriously at Harvard University, and figures in familiar red football colors (right) are often to be seen on the playing fields.

The University sculling teams work out and race on the Charles River (right).

To many Americans, Memorial Day is a time for picnics and beach parties. But for others, it is a day to remember old friends who didn't come back from their country's wars.

Cape Cod is a
wonderland of colorful
cranberry bogs (left), of
seagulls and fishing fleets
(above), and long, quiet,
sandy beaches (below),
ideal for bracing walks to
refresh the spirit.

Boston's Quincy Market (right) dates back to pre-Revolutionary days – but happily the quiche does not.

How can you participate in a swimming meet without getting wet? Be a timekeeper (right), of course.

No, this is not Paul Revere, but a Boston mounted policeman, who can tell you where Revere's house is.

In Old Sturbridge Village, a living museum, costumed guides conduct visitors (below) through the past, often in transport of the last century. In this wooded haven, time moves as slowly as the horses.

Feeling hungry? Perhaps a giant Boston pretzel will fill the void for you. And don't forget the mustard!

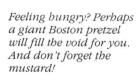

The open waters of nearby Block Island Sound (right) attract the sailing enthusiasts.

When the sun comes out in Westerly, folk head south for Misquamicut State Beach (below).

Sand and sky of Misquamicut Beach bathed in evening's golden light.

The snack bar is closed, but who cares? The line forms to the right anyway.

In Newport they still build boats (above) the old way.

Newport (below) is still a fishing town and the catch of the day remains important.

For a more exposed way to catch the sea breezes, try a hand-finished sailboard (right).

Newport Casino's Tennis Museum and Hall of Fame is also a place where croquet is played. Oscar Wilde was one of the Casino's distinguished visitors.

Are they biting? Does it matter? He could feed on the memories taken home from such a place.

Ships no longer depart from Mystic Seaport, now a museum village, to go whaling, but visitors can explore the magnificent 1841 whaler, Charles W. Morgan *(below), which made thirty-seven voyages, from the South Seas to the Arctic, in her time. Standing beneath the mast, it is easy to imagine yourself bound for Cape Horn.*

Henry C. Bowen was famous for his Fourth of July picnics, held at Roseland Cottage (right), his Gothic Revival home in Woodstock. Four presidents were guests at these picnics: Grant, Hayes, Harrison and McKinley.

To prepare for their own Independence Day cookouts, Sherman folk need look no further than their local hardware store (left).

On New Haven Green, the campus of Yale University (right) is not covered with ivy, but it is in the right league.

Men of many parts, young hopes for the Yale rowing team must also get through school.

In the old days, students dressed up to go to classes, and the old Yale fence (right) depicts those days of student finery.

Looking for anything from a job or a bit of fun to a lost dog makes the Yale student bulletin board (left) some of the most important reading on campus.

Students seem to be getting younger-looking every year ....

Balloon trips (above) could give your body and spirits a lift, skimming the tops of the trees over the Connecticut countryside.

Below: New Haven parades its historic past. Fortunately, the Foot Guard Band of 1775 will only suffer from foot fatigue, not battle fatigue.

Little League (right) isn't for small-timers. Who knows? these sluggers might even make it to the World Series.

Catch a streetcar (above) into the past at the Trolley Museum in East Windsor. Some of the cars date back as far as 1894.

On a crisp autumn afternoon in the Connecticut hills, a father and son and their faithful companion set out on the trail of varmints.

If Rip van Winkle, on awakening from his twenty-year sleep, had stumbled on this Catskill camp (left) he might have felt more in tune with the times.

On the other hand, if he had wandered near this tranquil mountain waterfall (above), he might have been lulled back to sleep.

But, in fact, he went back to the Hudson River Valley (below).

Facing page: the Hudson River at sunset.

A uniform alone does not make a soldier.

The Military Academy at West Point (below) has produced world-famous soldiers.

Even today, the Statue of Liberty has an important message for us all.

The Manhattan skyline never fails to make an impression.

In Spanish Harlem, wedding fiestas, beginning at the church (above), go on long into the night.

A smiling traffic warden?

Left: an old woman sits in the doorway of a Little Italy wine store.

On the streets, amid the constant chaos of Big Apple traffic, intrepid messenger men, as brave as the runners of old, deliver important packages.

A commuter train journey (above) is probably the least stressful way to begin a day's work in New York and it enables the financier to catch up with the Wall Street Journal.

The sidewalks of New York seethe to music of all sorts, from jazz with a swing to music with a soul and a cause.

When the sun comes out, hundreds of New Yorkers bare their winter-white bodies to the sun in Central Park (above).

New York's Central Park is a great place to paint a picture (left).

Relatively secluded from the metropolitan hubbub, Central Park is also a perfect place to catch up on some reading (below).

In Central Park, it is not only politicians who kiss babies.

The Park is an oasis of greenery in the middle of the city (below).

*The lobby of the
Algonquin Hotel on 44th
Avenue – between Fifth
Avenue and the Avenue
of the Americas, is a
perfect starting point for
any New York City
adventure. Here, in the
1920s, Alexander
Woollcott formed the
famous "Round Table,"
which included Robert
Benchley, Dorothy Parker
and Robert Sherwood.*

*Imaginative window
displays make shopping
in New York is just as
much fun when the stores
are closed.*

Amid the riches of New York City, there is a great deal of poverty and dereliction.

New York's Orchard Street (left) is the place to find a bargain any day of the week except Saturday.

The permanently congested City avenues (below) are enough to make some people wonder how all the cars, cabs, trucks and bicycles manage not to end up in an immovable knot of traffic.

The New York Chinese join in American-style celebrations (right), at the same time maintaining their own culture.

The largest community of Chinese outside the People's Republic of China is in New York's Chinatown (below).

The Chinese brought their religions with them and Buddhists (below), for example, are not an unusual sight on the streets of Chinatown.

Chinatown has a real community atmosphere. The people know each other and curbside chats are a common sight.

The best way to see New York, they say, is from the water.

Among the finest sights in New York are the horses (left).

Not everyone is able to travel in such style. Perhaps some of the hapless commuters (facing page bottom left) awaiting the bus wonder if true horse power might not be faster.

When the fleet is in, the sailors (right) can hardly wait to go ashore.

Street musicians (below) provide all kinds of sounds on the sidewalks of New York.

They may even want to catch the Rangers playing hockey at Madison Square Garden (below right).

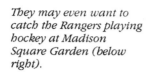

Above: mechanics on lunch break.

The Guardian Angels (right) are an independent peace-keeping force on Big Apple subways.

New York has its tranquil moments when the frenetic pace slows down and older citizens (bottom right) can watch the world go by in peace.

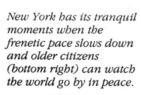

Even in modern New York, an Orthodox Jew (above) attempts to shun the trappings of the modern world.

New York's financial district (below) is like a huge concrete canyon of steps and high-rise blocks.

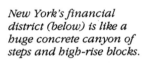

Sometimes the exhibits outside the Metropolitan Museum are just as interesting as the treasures on the inside.

No matter how hot it gets in the City, there is no need to go to the beach as long as there is a fire hydrant handy.

For the last few decades, New York's Puerto Ricans have formed the City's fastest-growing community.

A generation or two ago it was the Italian community that was expanding. Now the younger generation tends to move away from Little Italy (left).

For smaller people (right), it is a good idea to arrive early for the Puerto Rican Day Parade and save a roadside viewing spot.

Every year, for the five
days between Yom Kippur
and Sukkot, New York's
Lower East Side is host to
a Jewish "street festival."
Goods for sale are
lulavim, ethrogim,
aravot, hadasim and the
festival implements (left
and below) – all
necessary for the
celebration of Sukkot.

On the Lower East Side,
piping hot knishes are
sold fresh from pushcarts.

The weathered slabs of
stone on Brooklyn's
Brighton Beach (above)
give the beach a
refreshingly non-urban
atmosphere.

A butcher in Little Italy, serving a local community, escapes the pressures of big business and has time to sit out on the street and contemplate life.

Young New Yorkers pause to sit on a wall and have a snack. Sometimes, if there is no nearby wall, a man must improvise (below) …

Ahoy there! Is nobody going out for the Montauk (facing page top) shark hunt?

Paddle ball (right) is a popular beach sport.

There is no need to start your engines or bait your hooks. Just go over to Greenport (facing page bottom) and see what is cooking.

Worshipping the sun is an exact science on Long Island's beaches.

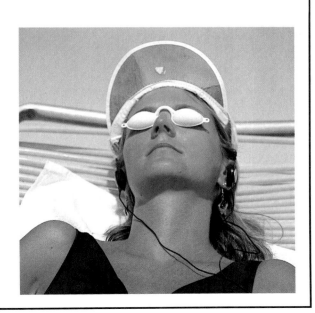

Most of Long Island's land has been divided up into building lots, but some farms still survive.

Horses in the Hamptons don't do farm work any more. They are kept for the delight of young girls and to provide exercise and pleasure for other horse enthusiasts.

"All welcome" is the appropriate declaration on the sign outside the First Presbyterian Church (right), which shares its premises with the Greek Orthodox Church.

There is a long tradition of winemaking in New York State, and this Long Island winery keeps glasses filled and tradition alive.

If anyone tries to make you bet that Niagara Falls (these pages) never slows to a trickle, save your money. Old Man Winter does the trick every year.

Of course, plenty of water gushes over Niagara's brink in the summer, and night lends it a different kind of beauty.

There are many places from which to view Niagara Falls, but perhaps the most dramatic views can be enjoyed by looking up at the falls from base level.

The Brave Old Army Team gets all the encouragement it needs from West Point's cheerleading team.

West Point Cadets (above) have enthusiasm to spare when their team takes to the field. Some band members even bring their unwieldly instruments with them to spur the players on.

When spring comes to the U.S. Military Academy, romance is not far behind.

Above: suburban housewives taking a break at the golf course.

In late summer, the thoroughbreds run at Saratoga (right).

"The sport of kings" is open to all those who love horses and own binoculars.

Eagle Lake (left), bathed in an evening shade of dusty pink, is one of the hundreds of lakes and ponds that riddle the Adirondacks.

Lake Placid (below), also in northeastern New York State's Adirondack Mountains, was made famous by the Winter Olympics of 1932 and 1980.

Only a day's drive away from New York City, in the Adirondack Mountains (right) lies the largest forest preserve east of the Mississippi River.

Lake Placid (below), for all its fame, is still quiet and peaceful, living up to its name.

Facing page: Western Pennsylvania, despite being the place where oil was first discovered and steel was king, is still a land of lakes and forests.

In historic Philadelphia there is nothing old fashioned about the firefighters (above).

Seen from the 330-foot-tall National Tower, Gettysburg battlefield (below), one of history's most famous fields of conflict, unfurls, dotted with hundreds of graves.

The "Phillies" in action at Philadelphia Veterans Stadium.

The fountain in Pittsburgh's Point State Park celebrates the confluence of the Allegheny and Monongahela rivers (left) at the point where they converge.

A "hoagie" is to a Philadelphian what a submarine or hero sandwich is to other Americans – but a bit different, and a lot better …

P.P.G. Place (above) is a shining symbol of the new, cleaner Pittsburgh. The glass facade is no mere architectural whim, it is an eye-catching advertisement for its owners, the Pittsburgh Plate Glass Company, and in it are mirrored its older, smaller-scale neighbors (right).

A statue of William Penn looks down on his city from the top of Philadelphia's City Hall (left).

Penn once walked along Chestnut Street (above), but there is not much about it he would recognize today.

Although it dates back to Colonial times, Penn probably wouldn't recognize Head House Square (below) either.

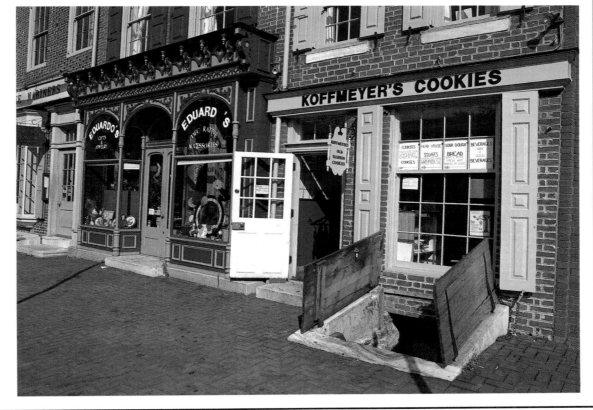

In spite of the few modern amenities permitted in some sections of the community, an electric stove for example, Pennsylvania's Amish families hold doggedly to their faith and traditions.

In Lancaster County, the Amish farms are tended the old ways and the sound of a tractor is almost never heard.

For the Amish community, a barn-raising is very much a community project.

The entire family is involved in running the farm, but there is still time left over from the chores for simple pleasures (right).

The neoclassical, cream-colored Philadelphia Museum of Art, with its columned portico is part of the magnificent city skyline to be seen from the Schuylkill River.

Lake Wallenpaupack is a 5,600-acre, man-made lake behind a hydroelectric dam in the heart of the Pocono Mountains.

At Presque Isle (left), during the War of 1812, Commodore Oliver Hazard Perry had the ships constructed that were used against the British in the Battle of Lake Erie. Things are quieter on Presque Isle now.

All is also quiet along the old Delaware Canal (above) in Bucks County these days.

The burning ball of evening's sinking sun sliding slowly towards the surface of Lake Erie (below) signals the end of a perfect day.

Atlantic City (above) is New Jersey's "Playground of the World," its "Las Vegas with a Seashore." The Boardwalk, with its famous rolling chairs, is still to be seen after over 150 years.

Farms (below) in the Atlantic City area continue to thrive, in spite of the urban changes going on so nearby.

New Jersey's past is still evoked by the Victorian aspects of old Cape May buildings (right).

Above: waving dune grass on the Jersey Shore.

Canoeing on the Delaware River (left) is a very popular activity.

If you think tuna is something that comes from a can, you have probably never chartered the Duchess (*left*) *off Barnegat Light.*

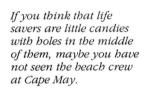

If you think that life savers are little candies with holes in the middle of them, maybe you have not seen the beach crew at Cape May.

A car in every garage was once part of the American Dream. On New Jersey's coast, that could become a boat as aptly named as the 2nd Dream *in every back yard.*

"Is this Granada I see? Or is it Asbury Park?" Off-season, Asbury (above) is a wonderful place for quiet walks.

The sound of surf crashing onto the shore is the perfect accompaniment to a long, invigorating walk along the beach.

A lucky roll of the dice could make you rich in an Atlantic City casino (left).

But please leave enough behind so Caesar (below) can pay his electric light bill.

The life of a stevedore (below) became a little easier and much more colorful when shippers started putting cargo in steel containers.

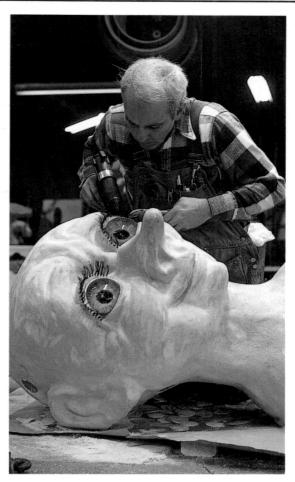

All New York turns out for Macy's Parade, but much of what goes into creating that spectacle is turned out by craftsmen (right) in Hoboken.

Harold Medina (above) has been going back to Princeton since '09, and it has hardly changed at all.

Some 400 companies are headquartered at Trenton (below), the State Capital and focal point of much of the State's history. It is a record good enough to make anyone walk tall.

As the nearest beach to Washington, D.C., Delaware's Rehoboth Beach (left) feels entitled to call itself "The Nation's Summer Capital."

Delaware's beach resorts began as religious camps. Now the only obvious sermons to be read are printed on T-shirts sold in the many stores (below).

The centerpiece of Harborplace, on Baltimore's Inner Harbor, is the U.S.S. Constellation *(right) – the oldest warship still afloat.*

Below: a farm nestled in the gentle hills of Maryland.

Commissioning Week at the U.S. Naval Academy (this page) in Annapolis is a time for celebration, culminating in the graduation of young midshipmen.

The Naval Academy was established at Annapolis in 1845 in a facility built initially for the Army.

Above: after that, a whole day's work lies ahead.

A working day in Maryland, as anywhere else, often begins with getting the kids off to school on time.

When the day is done, Baltimore's Inner Harbor (below) offers more than 130 shops and restaurants to be explored.

One of the most significant days in American history was April 13, 1743, the day Thomas Jefferson was born.

The charters of American freedom – the Declaration of Independence, the Constitution and the Bill of Rights – are enshrined in the National Archives (right).

Below: a formidable-looking statue of Ulysses S. Grant mounts guard at the foot of Capitol Hill on the Mall.

The National Airport (right) is less than three miles from downtown Washington – near enough to be in sight of the city's landmarks.

There are more parades and festivals in Washington than in any other American city. Some say there are more clowns too.

It is heady work keeping some of Washington's buildings clean.

Washingtonians certainly like to keep abreast of current affairs, and a picnic (below) without a T.V. set is perhaps unthinkable to many of them.

Indeed, should they be so absorbed that they forget their picnic lunch, the many street vendors ensure that that is not a problem.

Perhaps, a few decades from now, some of these women (above) will take out a dusty yearbook and wonder "Who was the girl with the spike on her head?"

Approximately 626,000 people live in Washington, and many of them cheer for the home team.

The names of 58,156 people who did not come home from Vietnam are inscribed on this black granite wall.

Most visitors to the Vietnam Veterans' Memorial are looking for a single name.

Many visitors go to the wall to remember the courage of the men and women lost in Vietnam.

In the words of Byron: "On with the dance!" (right).

A soldier guards the Tomb of the Unknowns in Arlington.

On the waterfront, fresh shrimp and other delicacies (above) are served with a smile.

Washington loves a parade (left).

The experts at the Smithsonian Air and Space Museum (left) know it as an Extravehicular Mobility Unit, but we would probably call it a space suit.

Dolley Madison, wife of James Madison, fourth President of the United States, was the first person to roll Easter Eggs on the White House lawn (above), and the tradition has not been neglected.

The original intention was to construct a Greek temple at the base of the Washington Monument. Instead, fifty "star-spangled banners" (below) surround it.

The Virginia planters and their descendents never lost sight of their British roots. Nor have the local foxes and hounds (above).

The Blue Ridge Mountains (left) are carpeted with blossom in the spring when the apple trees bloom.

*Above: the Blue Ridge
Mountains against a rosy
sunset.*

Below: the Potomac River.

The pale winter sun sets the Norfolk Botanical Gardens (above) sparkling with opal, platinum and silver lustre.

In spring, the crab fishermen once more plumb the depths of Chesapeake Bay (left) in search of its gastronomic riches.

Summer's sun entices hundreds to Virginia Beach to find a space on the sand.

*Virginians like to walk
hand in hand with their
history, and in Tidewater
country (left) the past
merges into the present
for many visitors.*

*Below: replicas of the
ships that brought the
earliest Virginians to the
New World.*

In Colonial Williamsburg, smiling staff (left and below), in the costumes of Virginia's earliest European visitors, welcome new visitors with old-fashioned hospitality.

Old Jamestown (above) lingers in 17th century.

The staff of Williamsburg and Jamestown are eager to share the past with everyone.

Mount Vernon (below), the graceful home of George Washington, is a sight not to be missed.

In the same day it is possible to take a leisurely carriage ride along Williamsburg's Duke of Gloucester Street (above) and then, later, to drop into "Shirt Shack" on frenetic, modern Atlantic Avenue (right), Virginia Beach.

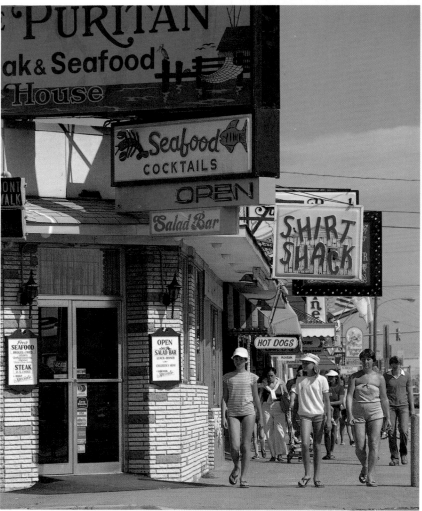

West Virginia is so rugged that even the Indians never settled in its mountains. But the men who eventually did (right) and mine its veins of coal would not trade those hills for any other spot.

Three states: Virginia, West Virginia and Maryland, and two rivers: the Potomac and the Shenandoah, meet at Harpers Ferry (left).

The 1826 Stagecoach Inn at Harpers Ferry (right) is now the visitor center for the restored 19th-century town.

Not all the money to be made from horses is made at the betting windows. Much of it changes hands at auctions (right).

Horses are serious business in Louisville (facing page), to the point of being honored on the town clock.

Below: harness racing at Louisville Downs.

The State Capitol (above), in Frankfort stands on a hillside, overlooking the Kentucky River.

Fort Knox (right), best known for its vaults full of gold, is also a substantial military post guarded by tanks and armored vehicles.

Burley tobacco (left) is the staple crop of the farmlands around Frankfort and Fort Knox.

Gristmills (below) still grind corn which will be mixed with pure water from limestone springs and used in the distillation process that produces bourbon.

The Ohio River (right) has always ensured the importance of Louisville.

Ashland's steel mills and oil refineries (left) blacken the landscape of the Kentucky highlands.

Even in downtown Louisville (above) there are fountains and pools in which overheated children may bathe.

The Belle of Louisville *(right) offers trips downriver in style.*

If you can throw your voice, 650 ventriloquist's dummies are waiting for you at Vent Haven Museum (left)

Below: a young man from Korea chews over the problems of citizenship.

Shakertown (this page) at Pleasant Hill is one of the few remaining Shaker communities.

The village's twenty-seven buildings are furnished with simple hand-crafted furniture and rugs.

The residents of Shakertown live just as the original Shaker settlers did when they first arrived in Harrodsburg in 1805.

It looks like an image from the past, but you can cruise the Mississippi tomorrow on this Memphis steamboat.

In Memphis, the choice of sternwheelers (right) is almost as wide as it ever was.

If you are not punctual the boat will leave the dock (left) without you.

Tobacco (below) is still one of the major crops in Tennessee.

Right: Burgess Falls near Nashville.

*"Elvis Still Lives!"
according to the tabloids.
Certainly, in Memphis,
his spirit will live on
forever.*

*"Graceland" (below),
Elvis Presley's Memphis
home, continues to
attract thousands of
faithful fans.*

Memphis was also the home of W.C. Handy, the master of the blues, who is commemorated on Beale Street (left).

Country music thrives in Nashville, especially at Opryland (above).

Any guitarist who plans to make his mark on the country music scene knows enough to take his guitar to Nashville.

The themepark (left) at
Libertyland, in Memphis,
numbers seventeen
different rides, each
giving a new perspective
on life.

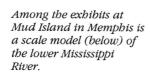

Among the exhibits at
Mud Island in Memphis is
a scale model (below) of
the lower Mississippi
River.

Right: two children play
outside an old shop in
Jonesboro.

"Is that the Chattanooga Choo-Choo?" Not quite, but it belongs to Chattanooga's Tennessee Valley Railroad Museum.

The Chucalissa Indian Village (right) near Memphis stands on the site of an ancient settlement established in 900 A.D.

In 1780, the British General Cornwallis called Charlotte (right) "a hornet's nest," a source of immense pride to Charlotte folk. Today it is more likely to be described as a hive of commercial activity.

Fayetteville (above), on the Cumberland River, although initially settled by Scots, was the first American city to be named in honor of the Marquis de Lafayette. Here, George Herman Ruth – "the Babe" – hit his first home run in professional baseball.

Old Salem (right), now part of Winston-Salem, was founded in 1766 by a small community of Moravians, whose homes have been faithfully restored and many form part of a living museum.

The world's largest cigarette plant, the R.J. Reynolds plant in Winston-Salem, keeps hundreds of farmers busy.

The Blue Ridge Parkway, leading to the Great Smoky Mountains National Park, runs past tranquil North Carolina farms (below).

These days it is not only the aircraft at Fort Bragg that have feminine names. The 82nd Airborne select the best, regardless of gender.

The folk of Hatteras Village (left) are said to speak in an accent still related to that of England's Devonshire, where the original settlers were born three centuries ago.

Parts of North Carolina's
Outer Banks are as much
as seventy-five miles, as
the gull flies, from the
North Carolina
mainland. It was in this
part of the world that
man learnt to fly from the
Wright brothers.

There are succulent crabs
waiting to be caught by
fishermen (right) in the
waters of the Outer
Banks, waters once plied
by the infamous pirate
Blackbeard.

141

How easy it would have been for Daniel Boone, a past resident of this area, to have explored the Blue Ridge by hang glider (below).

Perhaps an aerial view is the only possible way Uncle Sam (right) could gain any accurate conception of the enormity of his land.

The Blue Ridge Mountains are ideal for hikers (right) – although, in some cases, the spirit may be willing but the flesh is weak.

Left: hot air balloons floating noiselessly over the mountains into a golden sunset.

Flying or gliding is not the only way to find an aerial view of North Carolina. Hanging Rock (below) in the Sauratown Mountains, will provide a bird's-eye view of the countryside without involving take off.

Nature's own water slide is provided by the smooth rocks of Looking Glass Creek (above).

In Charleston, some of the South's finest and most elegant town homes are to be seen reflected in Colonial Lake (above).

More than twelve million people visit Myrtle Beach (right) each year, making it one of the busiest resorts on the Atlantic coast. Off-season, however, it can be a peaceful, unhurried place.

Some non-sunseekers prefer the shady solitude of leafy Charleston beside Colonial Lake (above).

Left: the long, smooth sandy stretch of the beach at Hudson's Landing.

Below: peaceful waterscapes at Fripp Island between Charleston and Hilton Head.

Parris Island is where the U.S. Marines train their new recruits. Before a man can be called a true "Leatherneck," he needs to learn some things about neckties (right).

Perhaps a more traditional, but none the less tough, military training is carried out at the Citadel (right), the Military College of South Carolina at Charleston.

Left: a recreated Civil War camp.

Clemson's Tigers (below) are one of the prides of South Carolina's sporting world.

Charleston's Cypress Gardens (left) are a 160-acre preserve of South Carolina's landscape.

It is possible to see baskets being woven on the streets of Charleston (above) just as they would have been a hundred years ago.

Right: the timeless charm of Charleston's younger generation.

Left: the Spartanburg High School Quintet prepares to perform at beautiful Rose Hill Plantation near Union.

The city of Atlanta (right) was less than thirty years old when the Union Army destroyed it – but Atlantans rebuilt it, and their building projects have not ceased since.

By St. Patrick's Day, spring is already in full bloom in Savannah (above), and so are the beauty queens.

The gold on the dome of the Georgia State Capitol (right) came from nearby Dahlonega, where there was a major gold rush in 1828.

The chain of subtropical islands stretching south from Savannah is known as the Golden Isles. They are famous for their beautiful white, almost tropical beaches (above).

In 1776, John Wesley, the founder of Methodism, preached on St. Simon's Island, probably on the site where Christ Church (below), in Frederica, was built many years later.

The Golden Isles form the sort of environment in which a front porch swing (right) is the most important furnishing of any house.

Above: going fishing.

Robert E. Lee, Jefferson Davis and, appropriately enough, Stonewall Jackson are honored in an extraordinary carving (left) in granite Stone Mountain near Atlanta, which rises 825 feet over the surrounding plain.

Geologists call this 150-foot-deep crevasse a "gully," but locals call it the "Little Grand Canyon."

Perhaps Florida's most famous attraction is Walt Disney World (left).

It is difficult to believe that Miami Beach (below) was once an all but uninhabitable, mosquito-infested sandbar.

Dolphin-skiing is a regular crowd-pleaser at Orlando's Sea World (left).

The deserted slips (below) off Holiday Isle give the impression the whole world has gone to sea.

Daytona Beach (left) is almost 500 feet wide at low tide, making it a perfect superhighway. Back in 1903, a world speed record of sixty-eight miles per hour was set here. These days, however, the beach has a speed limit of ten miles per hour.

Everyone loves the moon over Miami, but if you want to visit it, you have to start at Cape Canaveral (right).

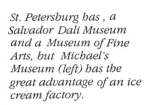

St. Petersburg has, a Salvador Dali Museum and a Museum of Fine Arts, but Michael's Museum (left) has the great advantage of an ice cream factory.

Sarasota is the home base of the "Greatest Show on Earth" and its greatest showman, Gunther Gebel Williams (below).

It takes four couples, to form a square, and a caller (right) to tell them where to go from there, and then the fun starts.

Bush Gardens at Tampa are known as "The Dark Continent." This thrill-producing ride is called the Python.

Florida's Hollywood Beach looks every bit as exotic as any on the Caribbean.

A fancy car is not usually of much use to anyone exploring the Everglades, but there are places where a driver can pull off the road to look for exotic birds, bobcats and even alligators.

The Carolyn Blount
Theater (right), in
Montgomery, is the home
of the Alabama
Shakespeare Festival.

The State Capitol of
Alabama (below) marks
the spot where Jefferson
Davis became President
of the Confederacy in
1861.

The Ave Maria Grotto
(left), at Cullman,
contains miniature
replicas of famous
churches and shrines
and is the result of a fifty-
year labor of love by a
Benedictine monk.

Fort Condé, a sixteenth-century French outpost at Mobile, is now staffed by soldiers in period French costumes (left).

Mobile (below) is Alabama's only seaport and, though it handles thirty-five million tons of shipping each year, it has lost none of its charm.

Power from the Tennessee Valley Authority has turned some Alabama farms (right) into factory sites, but many of the old homesteads are still standing.

Biloxi has been a busy resort town since the 1840s. The town's fine coastline is one reason for its popularity; streets lined with elegant houses (above) are another.

Cotton is still king in the Mississippi Valley.

Every port in America has its own tugboats, which don't only tug. Many are powerful enough to push dozens of heavy barges along the Mississippi (right).

A boat excursion on Lake Washington (below) is almost like a walk in the woods because of the cypress trees growing in the water.

Crescent City (above) has a brand-new look, but old-fashioned steamboats, such as the Creole Queen, *help keep New Orleans in touch with its past.*

Left: a New Orleans cowboy.

The old quarter of New Orleans (above), with its famous restaurants and delicate ironwork, is served by a streetcar, named Desire?

Horse-drawn carriages pass St. Louis Cathedral (right), Jackson Square, giving the area an old-world quality.

*What is New Orleans
(these pages) without its
music? It is everywhere:
in Jackson Square
(below), on the sidewalks
(right) …*

*Above: music stops the
traffic outside 700 Royal
Street in the Vieux Carré.*

When he was living there, William Faulkner probably heard music in Pirate's Alley (left) too.

Below: the traffic on Royal Street has no chance.

In just about any open space in town, New Orleans folk are treated to great music.

WARNING: THE SURGEON GENERAL HAS DETERMINED THAT CIGARETTE SMOKING IS DANGEROUS TO YOUR HEAL

*That is not "Big Brother"
watching you, it is only
the Marlboro Man.*

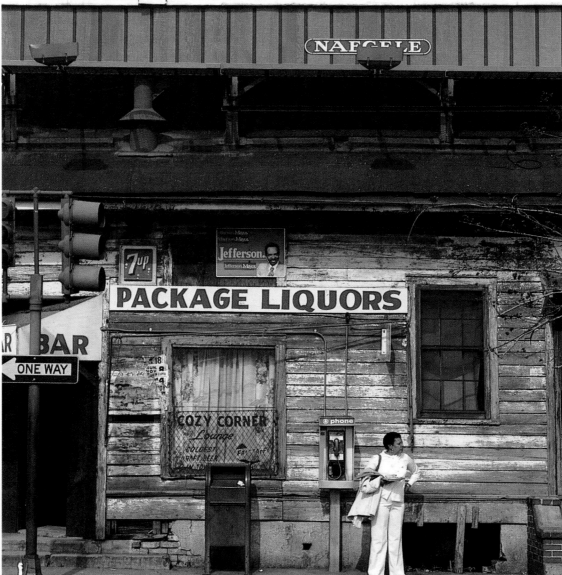

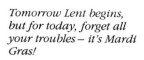

Of course, cowboy boots (left) might be a little bit more expensive, but a New Orleans shoeshine needs to make a living.

Tomorrow Lent begins, but for today, forget all your troubles – it's Mardi Gras!

Royal Street (above) is as good as any aisle.

When walking becomes too hard on the feet, a horse-drawn carriage (right) is a romantic alternative means of transport.

German Village, at Columbus, keeps its Old World roots well tended, especially during the Oktoberfest, celebrated on the State fairgrounds (right).

The Indians first chose the site of Cincinnati (below) as the best place to cross the Ohio River.

Thomas Worthington, Ohio's first Governor, lived in Adena, a Greek Revival mansion (facing page and right) at Chillicothe.

Below: cornfields thrive in Western Ohio.

The grisly trappings of Haloween (left) embellish Ohio's homes every year.

"A bird in the hand is worth two in the bush" says the old saw. Of course, to hold a golden eagle (above), the hand must be well-protected.

The Roscoe Village general store (below), in Coshocton, began selling dry goods in the 1880s. It has hardly changed since then.

Warren G. Harding, the 29th President, rejected the conventional speaking tour for a "front porch" campaign, making speeches from his Marion home (above).

Right: a pumpkin fair.

The landscape near Cheboygan was timberland when settlers first arrived. Extensive logging left it suitable for conversion to farmland (above).

The lighthouse (left) on Lake Superior at Marquette was rebuilt in 1867 and it is still in use.

The citizens of Detroit (below) are determined to make it America's most beautiful city.

Bavarian missionaries, hoping to make Christians out of the Chippawa Indians, founded the Old World town of Frankenmuth in 1845. Its name means "Courage of the Franks."

The 1957 Mackinac Bridge connects Michigan's Upper and Lower peninsulas. At five miles long, it is the world's longest suspension bridge.

The Henry Ford Museum at Dearborn covers twelve acres with its collection of vintage cars and other artifacts.

The Manistee County Historical Museum contains a reconstructed Victorian store of the type that served the community back in 1870.

Right: a tree-lined street in Sault Ste. Marie.

Houghton and Hancock, connected by bridge over Portage Lake (left), became boom towns when copper was discovered there in 1843.

Leland harbor (below) is a good place to set out from to visit Lake Michigan's Manitou Islands.

173

A speedy elevator whisks visitors to the top of the 284-foot-long shaft of the Soldiers and Sailors Monument to see the sights of Indianapolis.

The steps at the base of the Soldiers and Sailors Monument (this page) in Indianapolis provide an ideal spot to rest.

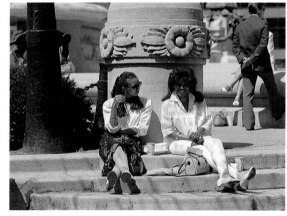

Monument Circle is not for sale, no matter what the sign says.

Chicago is one of the few cities where office workers can spend their lunch hour on the beach.

Chicago's lakefront stretches for more than twelve miles along Lake Shore Drive (left).

The people who work at the Chicago Board of Trade (below left) have commodity futures on their minds.

The masts of boats (above) bobbing on Lake Michigan set up a shifting skyline of their own against the towers of Chicago.

The Loop (below), with its office buildings and stores, lies in the heart of Chicago.

Right: the elegant State Capitol at Springfield in Central Illinois

The basketball team gets its "Go!" from its cheerleading team (above), whose members don't let little things like crutches dull their enthusiasm.

Nobody makes a move on the football field until the officials (left) have conferred.

Sometimes the cheerleaders (right) at a football game make it hard to keep your eye on the ball.

Right: lights in a fountain on a warm summer night.

The powerful rhetoric of an Pentecostal preacher causes young listeners (below) pause for thought.

Lake Geneva is more than just a place to take a dip. It is also a wonderful fishing lake and, in the winter, it is ideal for skating and ice-boating.

Lake Waupaca (left) is at the head of a chain of twenty-three lakes along which the possibilities for picnics are endless.

Below: Bayfield, on Lake Superior.

A convention of square dancers can build up big thirsts, but in Milwaukee, America's beer capital, that is hardly a problem.

Little Norway (right) was founded by Norwegian settlers at Mount Horeb in 1856. Many of its beautiful buildings have characteristic blue trimmings.

Left: young Wisconsin boys, dressed and ready, are keen to join the hockey match.

So many people fish for walleyes (right), it is amazing there are any still swimming.

Left: the Milkwaukee Art Museum, where art and nature converge.

Despite Wisconsin's winter ice (below), not many get away.

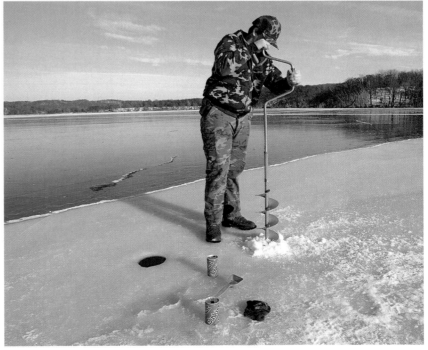

Traditional mid-nineteenth-century methods of building are still practiced on the Living History Farms (left) near Des Moines.

If you had an idea that Iowa consists of endless flat plains, you have not driven through Crawford County (below).

Among the five farms that constitute Iowa's Living History Farms is a typical 1900 spread, complete with a windmill (right).

The gold-domed Iowa State Capitol (below) stands on the outskirts of downtown Des Moines.

Daniel Chester French created a monumental sculpture (right), entitled "The Progress of the State," for the Minnesota Capitol building.

The Minnesota State Capitol (this page) in St. Paul is crowned by one of the largest unsupported marble domes in America.

Split Rock Lighthouse (right), on Lake Superior, was established to counteract the compass-confusing magnetic fields of the area.

The Baptism River (left) winds through steep gorges and past dense woodlands on its way to Lake Superior.

The Aerial Lift Bridge, which connects the mainland and Minnesota Point at Duluth (below left), can raise its 900-ton span in less than a minute.

There are more than
12,000 lakes in
Minnesota, including
Lake Nokomis (above) at
Minneapolis.

There is an acre of
parkland for every eighty
people in Minneapolis, a
statistic that includes
Minnehaha Park (left),
where Swedish festivals
are held.

Minnesotans are among the world's best sailors (above). It is no wonder, they have plenty of places to practice.

The Ukranian art of Easter-egg decoration (right) is preserved and practiced in Minneapolis.

Facing page: the Old Courthouse in St. Louis, framed by Eero Saarinen's Gateway Arch marking the starting point of the rush to settle the West.

St. Louis is the original home of Annheuser-Bush and Budweiser Beer, but there are many other kinds of beer (right) available.

The University of Missouri (left) was founded in 1841 with funds donated by ordinary pioneers. Its school of journalism was the world's first.

Above: the earth's bounty measured in carloads of golden corn.

Eureka's Black Madonna Shrine (left) is made of stones which once lay at the bottom of an inland sea.

Jesse James used Meramec Caverns as a hideout and, during the Civil War, gunpowder was made secretly in its five underground levels.

Modern machinery (left) makes the job of harvesting corn much easier.

Large tracts of Missouri are still covered in swamp (below).

Below: an armed pumpkin man sits as a scarecrow to warn off human trespassers who ignore the "private property" poster.

Thoroughbreds run at Oaklawn Jockey Club (right), Hot Springs, during the season, which runs from February through April.

Petit Jean Mountain (below) is named for a French girl who came to America disguised as a boy with her sailor sweetheart.

The Old Mill (above) at North Little Rock stands in a park that passed for land in Georgia for scenes in the movie Gone With The Wind.

Jim Bowie crafted his famous knife in this Ozark blacksmith shop (left).

The forest is thick in Little Rock's Pinnacle Mountain State Park (below).

Square dancing (above) is a favorite activity in the Ozarks.

Music-making (left) is part of the Arkansas heritage.

There are no oil derricks on the Tulsa skyline (above), a local law prevents it, but oil is what drives the city.

Downtown Oklahoma City (below) was founded on one of America's biggest oil fields.

The Arkansas River (right) gives boats from Tulsa access to the Great Lakes and the Gulf of Mexico.

Oklahoma was Indian
territory until as late as
1889. Cowboys began the
settlement process, and
raising cattle (above) is
still important.

Tulsa's Philbrook
Museum of Art (below) is
housed in an Italianate
villa set in a twenty-three-
acre park.

In 1830, the so-called "Great White Father" relocated five Indian tribes to the Oklahoma Territory. Today the state contains the country's largest Indian population.

The Indians of Oklahoma maintain their culture and traditional rituals (left).

Below: the cowboy way of life is also thriving. A young girl (above) would learn to ride at an early age.

There are three Indian tribes living on reservations in Texas, including the Alabama-Coushotta (above), who live near Houston.

Houston (below) began to expand in 1836, the year the Republic of Texas was established.

The Lyndon B. Johnson Space Center (left), along with the Space Age Museum and the National Aeronautics and Space Administration – N.A.S.A. – souvenir center, have earned Houston the title "Space City."

Furthermore, the city is hard at work building structures (above) that themselves seem to reach for the stars.

Apparently unimpressed, the Rio Grande (below) continues to wind its way to the Gulf.

When Texans (these
pages) get together, they
do it in style – setting up
a huge encampment
(below) at Terlingua, for
example, devoted to
serious involvement in
one of their favorite
things: the Annual
Terlingua International
Frank X. Tolbert-Wick
Fowler Memorial
Championship Chili
Cookoff.

Broad smiles (left) wreathe the faces of Texans having fun in Terlingua.

The cookoff judges (below) have the serious task of finding the best chili in Texas.

The singing commancheros (above), many miles away in Josie's Gaslight Square in Corpus Christi, could be congratulating the Official Mouth (right), winner of the cookoff.

There are a few oil wells in Caddo Lake (above), near Marshall, but they are well hidden among the cypress trees.

Before the Anglos arrived, Texas was part of Mexico, and its Mexican heritage is still very much in evidence.

The ninety-foot-high, wave-like dunes of Monahans Sandhills, a state park, cover an area which was once a prehistoric inland sea.

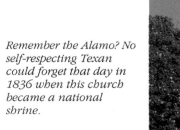

Remember the Alamo? No self-respecting Texan could forget that day in 1836 when this church became a national shrine.

Even by Texan standards,
the acreage of glass (left)
in Dallas is a window-
washer's nightmare.

The Hyatt Regency Hotel
and Reunion Tower
(right) are both relatively
new, but old enough to be
a well-known symbol of
Dallas.

Another much visited symbol of Dallas is Southfork Ranch, base of television's Ewing family in the soap opera Dallas.

Dallas is a long way from the ocean, but city kids can still experience pounding surf, simulated in a swimming pool.

If you thought all the clowns (left) were at the circus, perhaps you have never been to a Texas rodeo.

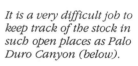

You will still find genuine "cowpokes" (above) at a modern Texas rodeo. Of course, most of the time they are hard at work.

It is a very difficult job to keep track of the stock in such open places as Palo Duro Canyon (below).

A cowboy's life has changed very little in a hundred years.

Texan sunsets have lost none of their power and beauty.

Out on the range, a cowboy (left) still has little opportunity to to let his concentration fail.

Longhorns are every bit as ornery as ever they were.

In Texas, not all the cowboys are out on the range. Some are on the gridiron at Texas Stadium in Dallas.

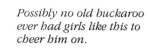

*Possibly no old buckaroo
ever had girls like this to
cheer him on.*

*Below: the Astrodome in
Houston.*

The Acoma Pueblo (left) has been occupied since 1150 A.D., long before fizzy drinks arrived on the scene.

This old Spanish church (right) at Taos looks surprisingly modern, but it was built in 1617.

The Taos Pueblo (below) features some adobe apartment houses that had tenants before America had a city.

White Sands National Monument (above) covers 146,535 acres of shifting dunes, which compose the largest gypsum deposit in the world.

When the wind kicks up the New Mexico sand, cowboys must go to work.

214

Turquoise jewelry and white face paint are part of the Indian tradition, but when the sun beats down, there are new ways to beat thirst.

The faces of modern Indians seem to be etched with ancient memories.

If anything can beat an ice cream cone it is two ice cream cones.

The Comanche (above and right) still assemble in all their finery to enact traditional rituals and dances.

*Views of the Grand
Canyon (these pages)
change from one minute
to the next as the sun
moves across the sky.*

*The mile-deep canyon is
eighteen miles wide at
some points, and follows
the Colorado River for
fifty miles.*

Bright Angel Trail (this page) winds eight miles into Grand Canyon.

It is a trip best made with an Indian guide (below).

But you may make friends (right) along the way.

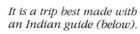

Some folk walking the Bright Angel Trail take along their own companions (below).

One of the most enjoyable ways to get to the bottom of the Canyon is on a three-day guided mule trip (left).

Wyatt Earp and his brothers took on the Clantons on October 26, 1881, in a gunfight at the O.K. Corral which made history and put Tombstone (right) on the map.

Unless your horse knows the way home from the saloon (above), better make that drink a sarsaparilla.

There are four museums in Tombstone, but the Wells Fargo Museum (below), with 75,000 exhibits, is the biggest.

Even before the sun comes up, the cowboy's day has already started.

Dance hall girls start young in Arizona.

From South Mountain, visitors are able to see a panoramic view of Phoenix (below).

There are six Indian tribes in Arizona, but the best-known and largest of them is the Navajo (left and right).

Navajo jewelry is very popular with visitors to the Southwest.

The Navajo National Monument (above) includes three prehistoric cliff dwellings.

There are about 160,000 Navajo Indians (this page) on their 25,000-square-mile reservation.

In 1800, the Navajo were forced to leave New Mexico, but sixty-five years later they were allowed to go home again.

The Hopi Indians (this page) have lived in what we call Arizona for more than a thousand years.

Their reservation near Flagstaff is completely surrounded by the Navajo Reservation.

They stage frequent pow-wows and, once in a while, an all-Indian rodeo (right).

White House (left) is one
of sixty ruins in Canyon
De Chelly National
Monument, and was
occupied as early as
1060.

How long can he stay on?
Every precarious moment
seems like forever in a
rodeo (below).

Saguaro cacti, the state
flowers of Arizona, can
grow as tall as sixty feet,
but they take as many as
200 years to reach such
heights.

The North Dakota State Museum at Bismarck provides the visitor with a detailed documentation of the history of the northern plains.

Patterson Reservoir (facing page), near Dickinson, is part of a Missouri River reclamation project.

Williston (below) was given up for dead after the droughts of the 1930s. Now the town has taken on a new lease of life.

Bonanzaville, U.S.A., at Fargo contains more than forty-five historic buildings, including two cabins (above), one with a second story.

Theodore Roosevelt once lived near Medora (below) and had a financial interest in the still-operating general store.

The State Capitol (above) at Pierre is built from granite quarried nearby.

Rapid City (below) was built to provide ways for gold miners to spend their money. It is hoped that visitors will do likewise.

Gutzon Borglum began carving presidents' faces on Mount Rushmore (above) in 1927. He was still finishing off the work when he died in 1941.

The Badlands (left), hostile-looking today, were covered with active volcanoes and roamed by sabre-toothed tigers a million years ago.

Stockade Lake (below) is one of four in Custer State Park, a game refuge that contains one of America's largest bison herds.

229

Main Street in Gordon (above) was part of the route Pony Express riders used across northern Nebraska.

Omaha (right) is the world's biggest livestock center and the home of the Strategic Air Command.

Working cowboys (this page) can still earn a living in Nebraska.

The state's cowboys play as hard as they work, and national rodeo champions routinely emerge from their ranks.

Pioneers headed West on
the Oregon Trail used
Chimney Rock (above) as
a landmark signifying
the end of the prairies
and the beginning of the
mountains.

Scottsbluff (right) was
another Oregon Trail
landmark, wagon trains
steering away from it to
avoid the hub-deep sand
by which it is
surrounded.

The countryside (above) near Ogallala was once the "Promised Land" sought by cattle drives headed for the railhead there.

Where longhorns once roamed, family farms (below) now churn up the ground.

Natives call this Kansas City (left), "KC-Kan," to differentiate it from "KC-Mo" across the Missouri River.

You can still catch a stagecoach at the Boot Hill Museum (right) in Dodge City.

Topeka was once a company town built as the headquarters of the Atchison, Topeka and Santa Fe Railroad. Now, of course, it is dominated by business of state and the State Capitol (left).

The chalky Monument Rocks (above), were formed by a prehistoric ocean.

At the gas station (right), further down the road, pop and frosty bottles of beer give welcome relief to overheated travelers at the bottom of the dried-up sea.

The cows still come home to Dodge City (above).

Harvesting (right) is a
machine-based activity
these days.

The state of Montana was
named for its
magnificent mountains,
but it is also carpeted
with prairies and miles of
wheat fields (facing
page).

Montana farmers do not
have much leisure for
golf, but the hat (below)
is always useful.

Out under Montana's big
sky, cowboys still rope
dogies (left).

The time for branding
brings the cowboys out to
round up the herds
(below).

Rustlers are rare these days, but a rifle might still come in handy out on the range.

Want to be a cowboy when you grow up? Why wait?.

These days, cowboys and cowgirls work side by side.

239

In its day, Virginia City (right) produced almost 300 million dollars' worth of gold. Now it is almost a ghost town.

Vigilantes once kept the peace in Virginia City, but now the sheriff (above) needs no help.

Old steam trains and vintage railroad cars are part of the history to be enjoyed at Alder Gulch (below).

Above: citizens of Virginia City share memories on the front porch.

Glacier National Park (left) straddles the Canada-Montana border, offering a panorama of dramatic views.

Vestiges of Montana's Wild West past are still to be found.

241

In the heyday of Silver City (right), there were thirty-eight stars on the American flag, but none was for Idaho, whose star was added in 1890.

By the time Idaho became a state, Boise had been its capital for nearly thirty years.

White-water rafting (below) is a sport that the old trappers on the Shoshone River could hardly have predicted.

Cowboys of the nineteenth century might not have believed that one day there would be an intercollegiate rodeo (below) at Cody.

In 1807, John Colter was the first white man see the breathtaking Grand Tetons (below).

Yellowstone National Park (these pages) was once Shoshone Indian territory.

When trappers began describing the geysers of Yellowstone they were thought to have seen a vision of hell and almost never believed.

Old Faithful geyser is almost as famous an American symbol as the Statue of Liberty.

The five national parks in Utah were established to protect natural treasures such as the pink limestone formations in Bryce Canyon (below).

Right: rock formations in Canyonlands National Park.

Left: the red arches of Capitol Reef.

Spectacular rock formations, such as the Sentinal (below) in Zion National Park, reminded early settlers of great cathedrals.

The 10,000-seat amphitheater (right) at Denver's Red Rock Park stages an Easter sunrise service and various outdoor musical concerts.

The Denver Botanic Gardens (below) are also used to stage outdoor concerts, to which the audience can bring picnic dinners.

The granite cliffs (right) near Telluride are best explored by jeep.

Below: the Denver Broncos light up the scoreboard at Mile High Stadium.

The Denver City and County Building (above) is part of a complex that includes an outdoor Greek-style theater.

Many visitors to Aspen (below) never see it without snow cover and miss the beautiful color of summer mountain scenery.

The Mile High City of Denver (above) began building upward in 1858 from a collection of miners' hacks.

Ouray (above) is known as "the Switzerland of America."

For eight centuries, the cliff dwellings in Mesa Verde National Park (above) were the homes of Indian farmers.

The Georgetown Loop Railroad (right) takes visitors on a spectacular seven-mile trip to explore abandoned gold mines.

251

In the Fort Smith saloon (below), Ridgeway, perhaps the dog days of summer are survived by thinking of snow

Maybe this thirsty sheep herder is thinking about snow too.

Some prospectors still pan for gold the old-fashioned way, but many miners, and cowboys, prefer to rely on more modern methods.

*The houses of Telluride
are an attractive and
colorful contrast to the
blanket of snow that
covers the town all winter
long.*

When the queues for the chairlift get too long, perhaps a horse (left) will do the job.

However, the views from the lift (above) are usually worth the wait.

Denali National Park (facing page), with a view of Mount McKinley in the distance, lends a new meaning to the phrase "winter wonderland."

Anchorage (below) accommodates 100 people per square mile, compared to New York's 23,494. Nonetheless, Alaskans like to refer to it as their "Big Apple."

Cruise ships are regular visitors to the waters off Alaska, but many Alaskans prefer to explore their waterways in smaller vessels (right).

Mendenhall Glacier (right) is a river of ice, fed by the 4,000-square-mile Juneau Icefield.

It is not usual for trawlers
(right) to arrive in port
decorated with balloons,
but there is nothing
unusual about its cargo
of halibut.

Glacier Bay National
Park (left) is best explored
from the water.

Above: the frost makes a man's beard prematurely gray.

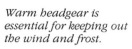

Warm headgear is essential for keeping out the wind and frost.

Camping on a glacier (below) appears to be a cold and precarious activity.

The layers of clothing must make it hard for a child (left) to put her hands in her pockets.

Living near the Arctic Circle requires some special dress codes (above).

Some of the views (below) make the heat privations suffered by Alaskans seem more than worthwhile.

Even indoors (right), gloves and boots are sometimes still necessary.

Perhaps bubblegum is easier on the Alaskan than a popsickle.

Seattle's Space Needle
(above) is 605 feet high,
overshadowed by Mount
Ranier, which towers to a
height of 14,410 feet
behind it.

Fun Forest Park (below)
in downtown Seattle
provides all sorts of
musical entertainment.

Many Seattleites prefer the
quiet verdure of Olympic
National Park (right).

There are more than 40,000 Indians, including the Lummi (above right), on twenty-seven reservations across Washington.

The Cascade Mountains (below) contain 300 glaciers and some of America's most spectacular alpine scenery.

Mount Adams (right) towers over 12,000 feet above Lake Takhlakh at the edge of the Gifford Pinchot National Forest in the Cascades.

His badge says that this fiddle player is a street musician.

Some pumpkins are just too big to get a grip on, but fortunately for small hands, they come in all sizes.

Japanese arrivals (right) in the Pacific Northwest have brought their culture with them.

Evening mist over the rocky islands of the Northwest coast (below) casts them in tones of charcoal, gray and silver, lending them a special air of mystery.

Portland's Washington Park, overlooking the city, contains a spectacular rose garden, and an amphitheater that is often the setting of outdoor concerts.

There are also rose gardens in Roseburg, but the town was named for a man, not the flower.

There are eleven waterfalls over as many miles in Mount Hood National Forest. At 620 feet high, Multnomah Falls, in the Columbia River Gorge, is the highest.

There are plenty of beautiful beaches (above) along the Oregon coast.

Left: sea lions catch the sun on a lazy afternoon.

If you want to find the fish in a biting mood, it is a good idea to be out on Lost Lake as soon as the sun comes up.

At over 11,000 feet high, Mount Hood (above) is Oregon's highest point. It is surrounded by a national forest covering more than a million acres.

Haystack Rock (right), off Cannon Beach – named for a cannon washed ashore from the wreck of the Shark – *is 235 feet high and overlooks a three-mile stretch of sand.*

Once they get their gear aboard the bus, will there be any room left for the children?

Crater Lake was once called Lake Majesty. About 7,000 years ago, it was a volcano.

Timber has been hauled out of the forests of the Northwest for generations, and there is still plenty of work for the next generation.

The idea of ever having to cut all those logs into boards manually is a thought that staggers the imagination.

Thirty thousand people once lived in Virginia City (above), and almost as many now visit there each year.

Even more people are lured by the bright lights and the idea of getting rich quick in Las Vegas (below).

But for some, there are cheaper ways to have fun, especially if they are less than elbow-high (right).

In California, where there are plenty of other things to do, thousands of people opt to run (above) twenty-six miles, 385 yards just for the fun of it.

Meanwhile, their neighbors are strolling along the strip (below) in Las Vegas, looking for a different kind of reward.

Pismo Beach (left) is the
only California resort
with ramps to get cars
down to the water.
However, some drivers
prefer getting there the
hard way.

Catching the waves at
Huntington Beach (right)
is the object of all surfers.

For the coast guard (below), plying the waters is part of the day's work.

Some visitors to Huntington Beach prefer to remain dry, catching sun rather than surf.

Right: offshore, roughnecks work long, hard hours so you can have a full tank of gas to get you to the beach.

Further up the coast, little tugboats scramble among floating logs (below).

You can walk up San Francisco's Fresno Street, but it might be easier to wait for the cable car to come back down for you.

Zig-zagging Lombard Street (left) demonstrates one way of overcoming the hill problems of San Francisco.

This is not the Celebrated Jumping Frog of Calaveras County, but he does a good imitation.

San Francisco's "Painted Ladies," its Victorian houses (left), are as expensive as skyscrapers.

If you are not overawed by the spectacular dragons (right), you will always find a warm welcome in San Francisco's Chinatown.

Hunger is not a problem in San Francisco's Chinatown (right). The only problem is deciding which restaurant to try.

Californians are frequently described as "laid-back," but nobody would say they don't know how to get a boot out of life.

What could express Californian individuality better than a one-man band?

San Francisco's cable cars are sometimes compared to roller coasters, but with an operator on board.

When you go to Fisherman's Wharf (left) for dinner, your compliments are due not only to the chef, but also to the crew who went out to sea to catch it.

Seagulls are the most dedicated fleet followers.

Foggy days make the skyline of San Francisco (above) look like a series of peaks pointing through clouds.

Sunsets through the fog (right) create spectacular light effects in San Francisco.

Even the fabled city of Oz would envy the beautiful jade color of Lake Tahoe's Emerald Bay (above).

Monterey's Cypress Grove is beautiful from any angle, but possibly most dramatic seen from Point Lobos (below).

Exploring the High Sierras on horseback (above) is as adventurous now as it was over a hundred years ago.

The Joshua Tree National Monument (below) covers an area of colorful granite formations and quartz monzonite boulders in southern California.

Without the sign, it would be hard to identify this spot as one of the most glamorous places in the world.

Beverly Hills is an
independent city,
complete with its own
City Hall (left), but is
entirely surrounded by
Los Angeles.

The sun-seekers stay on
the beach at Santa
Monica (below) until the
very last rays disappear.

There is more to do on Venice Beach (this page) than lie around in the sun.

If you do not want to get your feet wet surfboarding, skateboarding is almost as exciting.

For clowning around (left) or horsing around (above), California's beaches are stocked with golden opportunities.

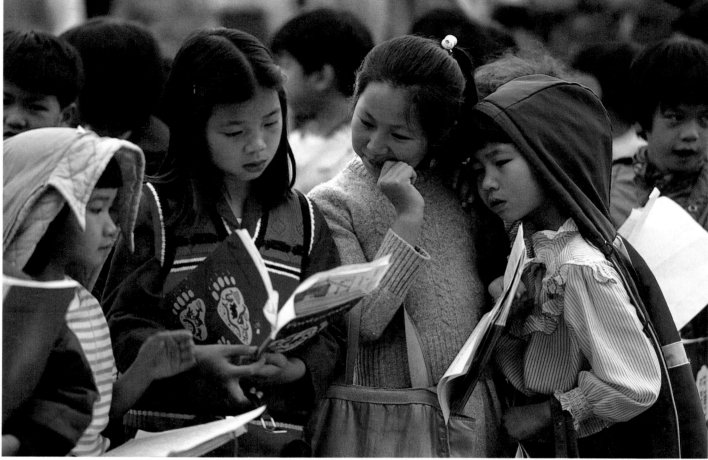

Four little maids from school face the age-old problem: "did you understand the homework assignment?"

No, this is not the movie set for Fifty-five Days at Peking, *it is a real part of Los Angeles.*

The life of a Californian offers all kinds of things to smile about ...

... and some things to make you laugh out loud.

"General Grant," the sequoia, is 267 feet tall and has a 107-foot girth.

The lake scenery in
Northern California's
Siskiyou Mountains (left)
could scarcely be
improved.

Below: a breathtaking
view of Big Sur.

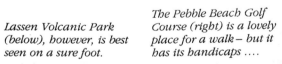

Clear Lake (above), in the
Los Angeles National
Forest, is clearly a good
place to tour on bicycle.

Lassen Volcanic Park
(below), however, is best
seen on a sure foot.

The Pebble Beach Golf
Course (right) is a lovely
place for a walk – but it
has its handicaps ....

*The Huntington Beach
lifeguards (this page) take
their job very seriously,
which must be why they
work so hard to keep in
shape.*

The Californian coast is perfect for sailing.

Redondo Beach does not cater only for the sun-seekers. Some of its visitors will be on the way to dinner at Fisherman's Wharf (above).

Below: Western Avenue, Los Angeles, lined with palms and posters.

Fans of the Dragnet *television show will recognize Los Angeles City Hall instantly as the place where Joe Friday worked.*

In those days, City Hall was the tallest building in town. Los Angeles has grown a great deal taller since.

Ronald Reagan held his out-of-town tryouts for the presidency here at Sacramento.

Do they really make California wine by stomping on the grapes? Does the camera lie?

Forest fires are the scourge of California, and almost a way of life for a Forest Service smokeater.

There are four windmills in the Danish settlement at Solvang and, of course, the best Danish pastry shops this side of Copenhagen.

Hang gliding (left) is a great way to get away from it all, if you manage not to land in a pumpkin patch (below).

A day without oranges would be like a day without sunshine – something almost inconceivable in sunny California.

Even in California people need to warm up (right).

A gift from the sea sometimes needs a little explanation (below).

Below: young entrepreneurs sell freshly made lemonade to quench the thirst generated by California's sunshine.

San Diegans refer to their city (these pages) as "the place where California began" – a claim that arises from the first recorded sighting of the site in 1542, nearly eighty years before the Pilgrims landed on the East coast.

The 11th Naval District is headquartered in San Diego, and many San Diegans are retired Navy people who now cruise the bay in their own ships.

The Del Coronado Hotel, overlooking San Diego Bay, has been the playground of film stars, tycoons and heads of state for more than 100 years.

The magnificent Casa Del Prado (above) is found in Balboa Park in central San Diego.

Above: Shamu, the friendly killer whale.

La Jolla (left) is also called "The jewel of San Diego."

Above: surrounded by a forest of ceramic insulators, an engineer keeps California's electrical systems in check.

Brush fires leave charred trees (below) in their wake, but Californians cope calmly with the problems of their land.

The distance from one McDonald's to the next is never too great, but perhaps it is a good idea to carry your own refreshments.

Right: an outrigger canoe race off Wailua Bay.

Facing page: waves crashing onto Kauai's cliff-walled shore.

Kauai boasts some of the most beautiful gardens in Hawaii, including that surrounding CoCo Palms Lagoon (below).

Kauai is perhaps most famous for its beautiful, white-sand coast (right).

*Fern Grotto (above) in
Wailua River State Park
is a favorite site for
Hawaiian weddings.*

*Opaekaa Falls (below) is
said to be the island's
most beautiful waterfall.*

The spectacular coastline of Molokai, "the Friendly Isle," is indented by Halawa Bay (right).

Left: evening light over the Kaluakoi area picks out footsteps in the ocher sand.

The Pali Coast (right) looks somber and menacing in mist.

Haleakala Crater is now dormant.

Surfing (above) originated on the South Seas as a means for Polynesian sailors to maneuver through surf to shore. It was banned in 1821 by European missionaries, who said it was immoral.

Taro fields (right) give an orderly appearance to valleys which would otherwise look wild with unrestricted growth.

Just about every hotel on the islands has a swimming pool, but none of them compares with nature's own (left).

The Lin Wa II *(right), brightly painted in natural vivid colors of Hawaii.*

Volcanoes National Park contains a variety of volcanoes, active and dormant.

However, the barren landscape to be seen from the boardwalk of Devastation Trail (above), created by a volcanic eruption, takes a long time to become fertile again.

The silversword plant (left), unique to Hawaii, is one of the first to grow on newly formed lava fields.

Of course, much of Maui's spectacular scenery (below) is shaped by volcanic rock.

A day's fishing off the
Kona Coast can produce
a marlin (right) beyond
your wildest dreams.

Hawaiians are famous
for their love of
celebration and dance
(below).

Captain Bean's
Polynesian Canoe (right)
offers visitors the chance
to see more of Kailua
Bay.

Waikiki Beach (below),
with its white sand and
clear water, is an
irresistable spot for sun
seekers.

The mountainous scenery of Oahu is spectacular. From the Pali Lookout a breathtaking view of the hills and sea unfolds (left).

Below: Diamond Head seen beyond downtown Honolulu.

The Byodo-In Temple (right) lies in the Ahuimanu Valley and is a replica of a 900-year-old temple near Kyoto, Japan.

Since 1937, Waikiki's free Kodak Hula Show has staged a spectacle of traditional Hawaiian dance in national dress to the accompaniment of ukuleles and guitars played by tutus, *grandmothers, wearing brightly colored dresses called* muumuus.

The "Pageant of the Long Canoes" displays a variety of Polynesian traditions: Fijian spear-brandishing, Maori legend and the Hawaiian hula *dance.*

Colorful catamaran sails
(left) also serve as
advertising space.

Below: Ala Moana Park
at sunset.

Sandy Beach Park (above) is a favorite haunt of surfers and swimmers who enjoy riding the waves.

Waikiki Beach (right) is one of Oahu's busiest, and the world's most famous, resorts.

Where would you like to be at this moment? Perhaps on a Hawaiian beach? Pick a spot anywhere "from sea to shining sea." The choices are endless in America.